FROM
MOUNTAINS
TO
MORALES

STORIES OF BOLIVIA

Windows Into Andean Culture, History, and Ecosystems

JEROME STEWART

FROM MOUNTAINS TO MORALES
Copyright © 2020 Jerome Stewart

ISBN (print): 978-0-9964879-2-4
ISBN (ebook): 978-0-9964879-3-1

Cover art: Alice DeSousa Stewart
Cover design: Sheila Edwards, sheliaedwardsdesign.com
Photography: © Jerome Stewart
Interior design & production: Domini Dragoone, dominidragoone.com
Editing & proofreading: Lynne Pearson, allthatediting.com

*For Terry Yates who introduced me to Bolivia,
and Silvya and Joseph who created Alice.*

Contents

Preface

Preface

Exit Ronald Reagan, Washington National Airport. Head out on I-395 which becomes I-95. Continue down, beyond the D.C. sprawl, deeper into Virginia. Along this route, somewhere between Springfield, Newington, Woodbridge, and Garrisonville, America shifts. Without borders or boundaries, the North becomes the South.

My wife, Alice, and I are familiar with this journey. As we have done many times, one summer afternoon not long ago, we drove this route to visit her mother who lives in Fredericksburg. An abundance of billboards lining the highway interrupted the scenery and ensured we were aware of the numerous fast food options available to us.

"More whoa, less dough."

"Hail to the beef."

"Eat Mor Chikin."

It was hard to tell that this same place, this suburban landscape speeding alongside our little rental car, was once a farm. Farther back, it was a forest. Once before, it gave itself to become the theater for some of the bloodiest battles of the American Civil War. Like the blood absorbed by soil that turned to dust, much of this history is gone. It exists in books, and the minds of a devoted few. The modern image of this land, our new America, is one of burger joints, strip malls, and an endless expanse of tract-home communities.

We exited I-95 heading west on Virginia State Route 3, which is also known as Plank Road, the Blue and Grey Parkway, and the King's Highway—although the monarch this name refers to was lost to us. We approached our destination, a neighborhood indistinguishable from all others save the names listed on street signs. Entering this suburban fortress, our surroundings hypnotized us—rows upon rows of tidy homes.

"I think we take the next right, and then a left after that," Alice said with unsteady certainty.

Were we on the right track? Caught in a maze with walls that reflected a limited hue of soft colors—powder greens, blues, and yellows—it was hard to tell. Everything looked the same—neat yards surrounding simple, well-kept houses. A quick phone call resolved our predicament.

"Mom, we're lost," Alice relayed.

"Ah well," her mother, Ms. Silvya, said.

Ms. Silvya, two words, always delivered together, is how I refer to my mother-in-law. This nickname, purposefully reflecting excessive formality coupled with suggested youth, is more of a brand.

"Ah well," she continued, over-pronouncing this common adverb, and making it sound like, "*bwell*." Her South American accent and mannerisms still overpower her English-language skills and North American habits, even though she has lived outside of her country for the better part of the past five decades. "Take a left on Rappahannock Drive, and then left on Hot Spring Lane. My house is fourth on the right."

After enduring the suburban labyrinth, we arrived at Ms. Silvya's house. She was waiting for us outside. Despite her full head of silver hair, she looked fifteen years younger than her age. Her home's ordinary exterior concealed her distinguished life. Items inside her home, many which she had obtained in bazaars and markets from across the globe, reflected her experiences and adventures. There were paintings and photographs honoring South American landscapes and people. There were other curious items including a hand-crafted chest of drawers, with wedges of light and dark wood, and accents of bronze carefully placed together to form arabesque designs. The chest was crowded with compartments that retained scents from Zanzibar, where Ms. Silvya purchased it many years ago.

Not long after we arrived, our attention shifted to dinner. Plentiful food is a constant when in Ms. Silvya's company. Her cuisine features an eclectic blend of tastes from around the world. There are Andean staples such as *sopa de mani* (peanut soup), and *papas a la huancaina* (boiled potatoes in spicy cream sauce). There are foods she learned while living in Ethiopia as well, spicy wat dishes served with injera. She makes everything with creativity and modesty. Long ago, Ms. Silvya learned how to stretch a limited budget.

After dinner, we moved to the living room for tea, and to inspect the assortment of cakes and chocolates Ms. Silvya had assembled for us. One bite, then two, and our bodies sank pleasantly into her couches. Fireflies with their green flickers of phosphorescence, the signatures of Virginia summer nights, danced in the backyard.

We talked for hours. Meandering between memories that spanned decades, the complete expanse of her long life, Ms. Silvya's stories began to settle on anecdotes from her earliest years. These stories, while reflecting cornerstone moments from her country's modern history, have gone largely unnoticed by most other people.

That evening in Fredericksburg, Ms. Silvya took us back to her childhood as it was lived in a distant and largely undisturbed part of the world nestled in between the Andes mountains and the Amazon jungle. She took us back to Bolivia.

Ms. Silvya's stories resonated with me. As a child, I listened to my parents' closest friend, Terry Yates, spin tales from his travels in South America. Terry was the head of the biology department at the University of New Mexico in Albuquerque, my hometown. His specialty was mammalogy, and Bolivian mammals were a focus of his research. From 1984 to 1996 he led a mapping of the country's extensive population of primates, cats, sloths, bats and rodents, funded by the National Science Foundation. Maneuvering through mountains, rivers and jungles, Terry and his team successfully surveyed much of the country, doubling the number of mammal species known to live there. By partnering with local universities and scientists, they helped develop the field of environmental studies in Bolivia, educating a generation of South American ecologists, geneticists, and conservation biologists.

Contemplating the plight of endangered species, and marveling at tales of encounters with tribes that have remained forever disconnected from the modern world, planted the notion travel would become a foundational component of my future self. I committed to one day immerse myself in things unexpected and unfamiliar. My most substantive early step in this direction occurred after graduating from college. Between 1996 and 1998, I served as a Peace Corps volunteer in Bolivia.

While countries in the developed world evolve in haste, the pace of change in Bolivia feels much slower. This is partially due the country's isolation—it is just one of two landlocked countries in the western hemisphere (Paraguay is the other). The slow pace is also reflected in Bolivia's economy. Despite immense mineral wealth, it is the second poorest country in the Americas, one notch above Haiti.

Bolivia is also politically volatile. Since 1900, control of the government has changed fifty-seven times. The number of military coups and countercoups closely parallels the number of democratically elected governments. With each regime change, incoming leaders promise citizens will be treated better, and the country's abundant resources will be better managed, to the benefit of its people.

While Bolivian political economics is often unsettled, the country's status as one of the world's most geographically and ecologically diverse nations is indisputable. Its landmass approximates the size of California and Texas combined. Within its borders, there are mountain goliaths towering thousands of feet above anything in North America, remote rivers tangling through the Amazon basin, and an almost unrivaled variety of plant and animal species.

Ms. Silvya is familiar with much of the country's geography as well as its history. For a short yet significant interval, her father led the Bolivian military. While his story has not attracted much attention outside of Bolivia, it provides a window into contemporary Bolivian politics—from the Chaco War pitting Bolivia against Paraguay, to the Bolivian Agrarian Revolution, to the arrival of Evo Morales.

Ms. Silvya's family's story is the basis for this book. I also include anecdotes from my personal experiences in the places her family once lived, as well as other locations I believe are relevant to attempts to depict Bolivia, its people, places, and past. This book is not intended to be a detailed historic reference, but instead a travel companion, for the adventures you take by plane, train, boat, and foot, as well as those adventures experienced while relaxing at home.

Map of Bolivia

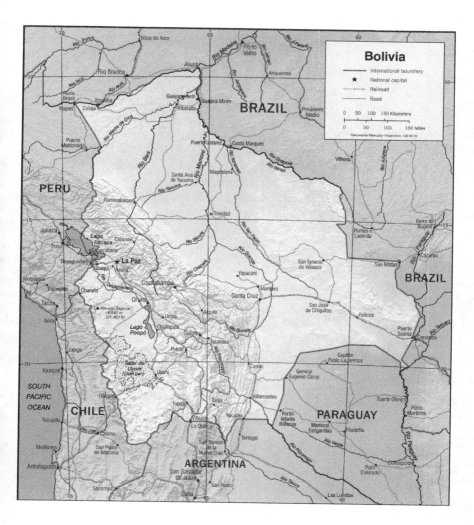

CHAPTER 1

My Introduction
to Bolivia

La Paz as viewed from El Alto with Mt. Mururata and Mt. Illimani in the background, 2011

"Our life is a hope which is continually converting itself into memory and memory in its turn begets hope."

—MIGUEL DE UNAMUNO,

DEL SENTIMIENTO TRÁGICO DE LA VIDA

I WITNESSED THE GRANDEUR of La Paz for the first time through an airplane window. After an overnight flight from Miami, the sun appeared over the Amazon basin. Minutes before landing, after the seatbelt announcements had been made, we were still flying over the jungle. Turbulence from a sudden shift in air pressure jolted the plane. Jagged rocks and ice became visible on mountain peaks that were so close I could make out detailed features. Then, seemingly without descending, we landed.

At 12,000 feet, La Paz is the highest capital city in the world. The city exists in a deep valley that is carved into a land of extremes. The Cordillera Real, the central core of the Andes mountains, defines the eastern edge of La Paz. Eight peaks approaching or exceeding 20,000 feet, guard the city. For decades, various geologists claimed either Mt. Illimani or Mt. Janq'u Uma as the tallest of the massifs in the Cordillera Real. GPS tools have recently put an end to the debate. At a towering 21,122 feet—Mt. Illimani looms above La Paz as the mountain king. Mt. Janq'u Uma rests to the north at a slightly lower height of 21,086-feet.

Legends tell of far more dramatic feuds between these Andean giants. Another peak from the Cordillera Real, 19,262-foot Mt. Mururata, which is recognizable by its plateau-like top, was once the grandest of them all. As the story goes, in a violent act of jealousy, Illimani chopped off Mururata's head. This crown toppled over and settled to become the 21,463 foot-tall, Sajama stratovolcano, also known as the Nevado Sajama, the highest peak in Bolivia.

Grouped together, the great peaks of the Cordillera Real create a barricade that the humidity rising from the Amazon basin is rarely able to penetrate. An ocean-like expanse of desert exists on the dry side of this barrier, expanding to the west beyond La Paz. This is the Altiplano, the South American high plain. At 13,000 feet above sea level, its altitude approaches the tops of the mightiest mountains in the continental United States.

Water is rare in this environment. Lake Titicaca is the most notable exception. Cut into the Altiplano, this is both the largest

Nevado Sajama, 2011

lake by volume in South America, and the highest commercially navigable lake in the world. Fed by the melting waters of Andean glaciers, Titicaca and the islands within it represent the spiritual and cosmological center of the local indigenous people, the Aymara, as it was for the Inca, and earlier for the Tiwanaku. This is where the sun, the moon, man, and woman were released to our universe by the Pachamama, the mother earth and mother time.

THE METROPOLITAN AREA that encompasses La Paz and the neighboring city of El Alto is the most populated region in Bolivia. It is also the country's commercial hub, administrative capital, and seat of the Bolivian executive and legislative branches.

The metropolis spreads from the valley floor along the Choqueyapu river, a stream that exists during most of the year as a subterranean watercourse, upward to the valley edge where the land abruptly curves and flattens. Mt. Illimani looms in the background. At night, the city lights are reminiscent of the molten lava that once cascaded down the side of this now dormant volcano.

La Paz residents are known as Paceños. Most live in precariously placed homes that fill a deep valley. These homes are often modest brick structures. Most are void of design aesthetic and appear to have been pieced together using a technique that champions utilitarianism as the primary objective. The exceptions stand out. Vibrantly colored structures with electric pink, blue, and yellow facades demand your attention. The color extends to the city's many markets with vendors selling almost anything—from food, to home goods, to witches' supplies. These markets crisscross the city's streets, scaling up the sides of the La Paz valley.

Most La Paz residents are indigenous. To not carry traits that were shared by Incan and pre-Incan ancestors would set a person apart. A Paceño man of indigenous origin—that is to say, the average Paceño—is around five-foot-three-inches tall. He is dark-skinned with jet-black hair. Paceña women of indigenous origin, who are also known as *cholitas*, are made measurably more distinguished by their attire. Their long and ornately decorated skirts, or *polleras*, cover simple petticoats. These *polleras* accompany brightly colored shawls, or *aguayos*, which feature tightly woven braids often made from the finest llama and alpaca wool. The quality of these *aguayos* rivals, and may even surpass, any other American textile. Accentuating this look—a bowler or derby hat. This accessory was borrowed from Englishmen who came to Bolivia to build railroads more than a century ago. The hats were too small for the men they were designed for. Undeterred by this detail, Bolivian woman adopted them, and continue to own this look. The complete Paceña wardrobe reflects a sense of self that is immune to outsiders' perspectives of image and style.

LOCALS AS WELL as visitors share a taste for coca leaves. Chewing wads of these leaves, or sipping coca tea, provides a mild stimulant that's similar in intensity to a cup of coffee. The feeling comes from a psychoactive alkaloid contained within the leaves. While it's true the Coca Cola formula once contained this ingredient, the drama surrounding this record and any stigma associated with coca leaves and coca chewing is excessive. The chewing experience does not compare to the reaction caused by cocaine which is extracted from a variety of the leaf after processing it with solvents and chemicals.

Coca chewing, or masticating—which is the English cognate of the Spanish word, *masticando*—is a cultural fixture; a ritual which has remained pure for thousands of years. The sooty remnants of ancient coca leaves have been found buried alongside Andean mummies. Pottery from pre-Incan dynasties depict people with conspicuously bulging cheeks. The descendants of these people continue to chew coca to make hard labor, hunger, and the extreme altitude more tolerable.

IN ADDITION TO the indigenous Paceño and Paceña population, there exists a small sub-culture of Bolivians with European ancestry. To classify these people as Spanish, Italian, German or of any sort of singular origin is misleading. Bolivia is a melting pot. For five hundred years, Europeans, Africans, and native South Americans have been mixing and remixing.

For most of the country's post-Colombian history, these lighter-skinned *criollos* have also been the ruling class. As children, they go to school together. They play together. Later in life, they work with each other. Then they marry each other. A bit later, they hire each other's children.

For the members of this privileged class, this selectivity turns large cities like La Paz into intimate towns with a few handfuls of family members, friends, and adversaries. These people congregate in homes and upscale apartments located near the city's historic central core—in the Sopocachi, Obrajes and Miraflores neighborhoods. More recently, they have begun to migrate deeper into the valley, down into the city's lower reaches, also known as the Zona Sur. This group of people has wedged a distinct taste of elitism into Bolivian culture, but their arrival has not displaced the customs and beliefs of the many cultures that preceded it.

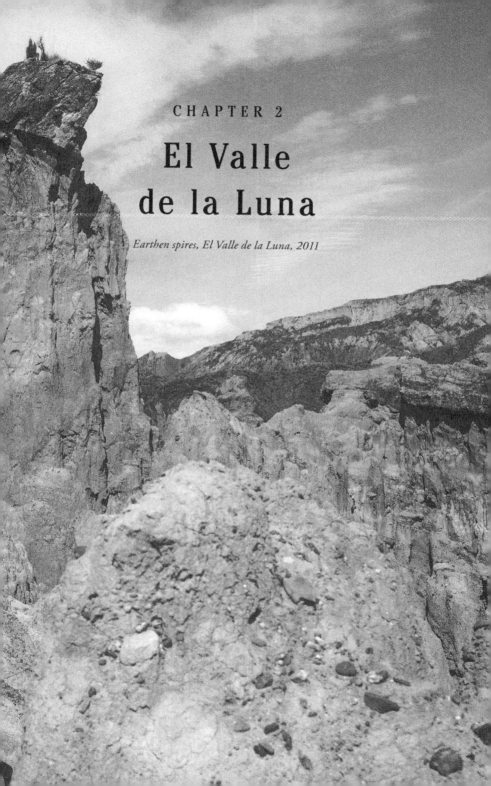

CHAPTER 2

El Valle
de la Luna

Earthen spires, El Valle de la Luna, 2011

> *"But when one is young, one must see things,*
> *gather experience...enlarge the mind."*

—JOSEPH CONRAD, *HEART OF DARKNESS*

DEEP INTO THE Zona Sur, about six miles south of downtown La Paz, there is a landscape that boasts an extraterrestrial allure. Rutted and gullied, yet accessible, el Valle de la Luna—the Valley of the Moon—is among the city's must-visit destinations.

The valley is largely devoid of vegetation. Of the few visible plant varieties, the Echinopsis pachanoi stands out. Known throughout the Andes as San Pedro, this cactus once existed in abundance in this part of La Paz. It has been clipped and uprooted by people—mainly tourists—who prize it more for its hallucinogenic properties than its rugged beauty and distinctive, columnar structure. A thin layer of flesh between the plant's waxy, protective outer shell and its inner stalk is the target of this harvest. Since the early days of Andean civilization, people have used this plant for its medicinal properties and as a pathway to commune with the spirit world.

While plants are rare, the Valley of the Moon features an abundance of earthen spires. The average spire has a diameter of around six feet. Many tower to heights of thirty feet or more. Some of the more prominent specimens have names. *El Sombrero de la Paceña,* or The Paceña's Hat, and *El Buen Abuelo,* or The Nice Grandfather, are two examples.

The spires are separated from each other by gaps as large as two yards but often as narrow as a few inches. They congregate around dark chasms that appear to be bottomless. The opportunity to hike, climb, and crawl down into these crevasses is the park's primary attraction. If the Valley of the Moon were in the United States, it would qualify as a National Monument. Visiting tourists would shuffle along well-marked and manicured trails. The park would be preserved as a sort of public terrarium. Contrast this with La Paz. When I lived in the city, the valley featured very few designated pathways. People were free to wander and experience, but also to touch and disrupt.

WHEN I FIRST arrived in La Paz, in 1996, I visited the valley frequently. I was attracted by the setting; a perfect backdrop for photo enthusiasts. Stones and minerals exposed to erosion and oxygen displayed an array of colors. The jagged rock formations provided texture and contrast.

On one memorable visit, I went there with a fellow Peace Corps volunteer, Pressly Albritton. His brother, Matt, who was on vacation from the United States, joined us. After a short *trufi* ride from downtown La Paz—which refers to the small minivans that form the backbone of the Bolivian urban transportation system—we were trekking among the crumbling pinnacles. Searching for the best photo angles, we scrambled toward the valley floor. About an hour into our excursion, rain clouds began to gather. Not wanting to get trapped in a gully during the storm, we decided to hike out.

While climbing, we noticed dark puffs of smoke gathering near the valley's upper edge. We continued to ascend to get a better look. Along the way, I paused to take some photos. Pacing a few steps behind Pressly and Matt, I made it to the top just in time to witness a mysterious-looking woman toss a black plastic trash bag over the valley's edge.

"She placed two live rabbits in that bag!" Pressly said. Confused yet curious, we glanced around and found the woman standing on a small plateau a dozen or so yards away from us. She was positioned next to another woman and a young boy. The three of them were singing or chanting in the middle of a triangle formed by small fires burning at its points. The bag of bunnies rested on a ledge about thirty feet below, caught between crumbling spires.

MOST BOLIVIANS ARE Catholics. They go to mass on Sundays and holidays. Yet traditional ceremonies and rituals, deeply rooted in the pre-Christian faiths of the indigenous peoples, continue to play a significant role directing their modern society. The blending of Christian and pagan practices reflects the clash of cultures that has characterized Bolivia for five centuries.

In the markets of La Paz and other towns across the Altiplano, you can easily find items and idols intended for pagan ceremonies. There are sweet-smelling herbs and incense, and light-hearted trinkets including gold-colored sapos, or lucky frogs, and *Ekeko* statues, which are miniature figures of grinning men with their fists full of cash. There are gloomier items too—ornamental sacrificial knives crafted from stone or bronze along with large quantities of llama and alpaca fetuses, which as I've heard, result from miscarriages.

People collect these items with plans to burn or bury them to commemorate an event which can be a birthday, an anniversary, or a purchase. They also do this to ward off sickness, or with hope they will someday achieve some wish.

Uniquely Bolivian holidays reflect these pagan roots. These include *El Día de las Ñatitas*—the Day of the Nose-less, or the Day of the Skulls. This holiday occurs annually on November 8th. Not to be confused with *Dia de los Muertos*, or Day of the Dead, which in Bolivia starts on October 31 and continues through November 2, or *Todos Santos*, All Saints day, which happens on November 1, the Day of the Skulls is distinct. Adherents decorate human skulls with flowers and clothing. They feed the skulls tastes of alcohol along with a continuous supply of cigarettes—a selection of items the deceased are suspected to be missing.

What's remarkable is that these skulls are typically from strangers. They were purchased in a shop, received as gifts, or discovered in some cemetery. The arbitrary relationship between the skulls' present owners and the souls that once inhabited them defines the moment. These are the remains of the forgotten. Celebrating and honoring them reflects the society's broad appreciation of ancestry. Believers also claim the skulls possess magical qualities. They believe the deceased communicate through their dreams. The skulls become their family. They are their brothers and sisters, sons and daughters. In exchange for the love and friendship they receive, devotees protect the skulls, and the skulls protect them.

Live sacrifice is another example of a still vibrant, yet ancient, Andean ritual. Centuries ago, the people who populated present-day Bolivia sacrificed llamas, alpacas, as well as humans to honor the Pachamama. Today, humans are mostly spared (we'll revisit this toward the end of the book.) Animals, conversely, are sacrificed regularly to ensure vibrant crop yields, successful marriages, and happy homes.

While they are remnants of ancient traditions, these activities continue to reflect Bolivians' deeply rooted relationship with their land. Long before Catholic priests and nuns, and evangelical preachers existed in this part of the world, shamans—intermediaries between life and the afterlife—were the key practitioners of local faiths.

THAT EXPERIENCE IN the Valley of the Moon with the bunnies in the bag was my first with these Andean rituals. While I was taking pictures a few steps behind them, Pressly and his brother were witness to the full episode.

"Those women cleaned that boy with the rabbits," Pressly said. "He was standing in the center of that triangle with his arms stretched out. The women were rubbing the bunnies all over him."

Having absorbed whatever it was that needed to be cleansed, the rabbits were placed into the plastic bag, and tossed to their fate. As Pressly retold the story, the ritual continued. The boy had stepped out of sight, but the women remained. After completing what appeared to be a dance, they brushed each other with a new pair of unidentifiable white-colored balls. Perhaps these too were small animals?

The women were preoccupied, or otherwise unbothered by our presence. We turned our attention away from their sermon to the bag and its furry contents. It lay motionless below us. As a first step, a predictable test issued by twenty-something-year-old boys, we tossed a few small rocks at it.

At first, nothing. Then the bag began to wiggle.

Fearing the sack had been targeted with some form of hex, we hesitated. Then, bravely, Pressly pulled out his pocketknife. In reflection, I don't think this had any use other than to symbolically imply he was ready. Together, we made our way back down into the valley, hoping to save the rabbits.

Upon our arrival, I held back and watched as Pressly sliced into the plastic. Two docile but unsteady creatures poked their heads out. Grabbing them by the scruff, we placed them on a rock. I hoped they would hop away, but they had lost their spring. We put them snuggly into Matt's backpack, and then scrambled back up the cliffside.

After reaching the top of the valley's edge, we noticed the women had left. The triangle, marked by its small fires, continued to smolder. We walked over to investigate. Three fires burned inside of small pots. These were *ch'allas*, or offerings. (The indigenous Aymara language word, *ch'alla*, is spelled with an apostrophe after the first syllable to imply an explosive sound.) We found an intact chicken's egg on top of each of these *ch'allas*. These eggs must have been the enigmatic white balls the women had used to cleanse the boy.

As if we had disrespected an unknown yet powerful force, the sky burst open. Hail pelted us, and splashed mud up our legs. Poor conditions and the trauma of witnessing an attempted rabbit sacrifice encouraged us to leave. We made our way back to the road and hailed another *trufi*. From inside the humid and musty minivan, we checked on our furry companions.

The black rabbit, still stunned with shock, panted away. The white one was motionless.

"I think he's dead," Matt whispered.

"He's probably just a little scared," Pressly replied.

Despite the wishful prognosis, Matt was right. The little white rabbit had escaped one fate, only to fall victim to another.

The driver stopped the *trufi* to allow us out. There, on a bridge next to the Choqueyapu river, we released the white rabbit into the stream. Then we made our way back to our apartment in La Paz with the remaining rabbit survivor which we named Luna. A few weeks later, another Peace Corps volunteer took Luna to his site in the Bolivian *campo*, the small town of Luribay, located a few hours outside of La Paz. I presume the rabbit's descendants still live there.

MYSTERIOUS RITUALS AND grand cultures have emanated from Bolivia. The country's history, nonetheless, has remained unfamiliar to most people. For the most part, what has happened in Bolivia has stayed in Bolivia. And so, it has been with Ms. Silvya's family—the Torres-Sanjinés family. A locally prominent and influential group, their lives with all the ups and downs, have remained preserved, like a jewel within a rock awaiting discovery.

CHAPTER 3
La Paz & Sucre

Mt. Huayna Potosí, 1996

*"All the regions of the globe have contributed their
fruits and abundance to adorn and enrich this
quarter part of the world which we Spaniards
found so poor and destitute of the plants and
animals most necessary to nourish and give service
to mankind, howsoever, prosperous and abundant
the mineral resources of gold and silver."*

—FATHER BERNABÉ COBO, *HISTORY OF THE INCA EMPIRE*

M S. SILVYA'S FULL name is Silvya Gladys Angelica Torres Sanjinés. She was born in La Paz on February 18, 1937. She spent
her early life in always formal and sometimes elegant homes in the
city's most historic and centrally located neighborhoods. Most of her
childhood memories feature her sister, Gloria, and brother, Gustavo,
along with their twenty-two first cousins. While other memories
have faded with the years, the times she spent with her family are
preserved in detail. "I don't remember many other friends," she said,
"or having the time to spend with them." Engagements with such a
large and close family provided a wealth of anecdotes—comedies
and dramas too—that have helped fuel her longevity.

Silvya's mother, Alicia Sanjinés Vidaurre, was born in La Paz
in June 1902. Silvya described her as bright and loving as well as

a devout Catholic. Her interpretation of the word of God, coupled with the standards conceived by the society she was a member of, served as her life guide. Alicia was also emotive, and deeply connected with the environment, people, and creatures that surrounded her. She loved animals and welcomed pets of most sorts into her world. Throughout her life, she was surrounded by dogs, birds, and occasionally other creatures that had been orphaned, or otherwise acquired, from the Bolivian jungle.

Alicia's father, Crisologo Sanjinés, was tall and slender. He always wore a suit, and typically was adorned with a brimmed hat. His prominent Roman nose provided a testimony to his European ancestry. At the base of this nose, Crisologo flaunted a mustache. Not just any mustache, and not one that he intended to go unnoticed, his version had two pointy ends. Twice daily, in the morning and afternoon, he retreated to a washroom to wax these points to sharp perfection. Tailored and smart, a man to be reckoned with, Crisologo looked the part.

The type of gentleman-class Crisologo represented began to go extinct around the time he was born. By profession, he was a landowner, purchaser and purveyor, as well as a locally prominent agriculturist. He kept himself busy, and to a degree removed from his family, by methodically managing and organizing his personal affairs. This occupation entailed reading newspapers and attending meetings with his friends and associates for coffees and gossip. His profession also encouraged him to regularly visit his beloved *finca*, or farm, in the Yungas, a high-altitude cloud forest a few hours' drive from La Paz.

The *finca* provided Crisologo and his family with an escape, a retreat to a simpler time. It encompassed several hundred acres of land near the Unduvai river, which is well-known for its abundant supply of trout. Typically, the family accessed the *finca* by horseback. Some parts were reachable by foot, but only for people carrying machetes. The ever-lush plant life quickly consumed freshly cut trails along with any other unattended artifact.

The family's home on the *finca* was restful yet rustic. It had two levels, but no running water or electricity. On the top level, there were simple living quarters with metal-framed beds and straw mattresses. Horses and livestock were stabled on the bottom level. Food was prepared in a separate building. Between this building and the main home, there was an expansive patio with a well for drinking water, and a large, tiled surface for collecting and processing produce cultivated on the property.

Despite its primitive aspects, or arguably because of them, the *finca* was a wonderland. It traded buzzing city streets for tangled trees filled with the sounds of songbirds, howler monkeys, and chirping insects. All of this surrounded by an almost incomparably lush and diverse vegetation.

Crisologo employed an assemblage of local laborers. They lived on the *finca* and performed all the tasks required to keep it running and vibrant. The fruit, coffee and coca they cultivated, coupled with the money Crisologo earned from periodically buying or selling land, supported his family.

THERE ARE FEW remaining details about Crisologo's first wife, Alicia's mother and Silvya's grandmother, Angelica Vidaurre. She came from an affluent family and a segment of society that prized women for their outward appearance, as well as their ability to maintain composure.

Angelica died from an unknown cause at a young age. Incapable of raising his family alone, Crisologo remarried. His second wife, Carmen, quickly fit into a comfortable maternal groove. While Alicia and her six siblings—Filomena, Criso, Julio, Betty, Alina and Marina—forever maintained distance from their father—intuitively addressing him with formality, reverence, and a touch of fear as, *usted papa*—they sustained a friendly and informal connection with their stepmother, referring to her as Mama Carmen.

The family lived in a stately Victorian home on *calle* Ingavi near a prominent intersection with Avenida Montes, the boulevard slicing the city in two. (Today, this intersection features a prominent pedestrian bridge connecting the Plaza Murillo-side of La Paz with the Plaza San Francisco-side.) The house was also located close to *calle* Jaen, a narrow cobblestone road lined with buildings boasting white-washed walls and seemingly a chapel on every corner. A walk down *calle* Jaen would transport you back to old Bolivia.

Since it was first constructed over a century ago, the house has retained a prominent position in the city's architectural portfolio. While living in La Paz, I became familiar with it, not intimately, but well enough to become surprised when I learned many years later that it was where my wife Alice's grandmother grew up. One of my apartments (because I lived in three apartments while in La

Crisologo's home on calle Ingavi, 2011

Paz) was also on *calle* Ingavi, one block away from this home. I recall its decorative façade and protruding windows with cast iron accents. An air of nobility seemed to elevate the home above its surroundings.

FOR SILVYA, HER siblings, and their cousins, the family's home, or Crisologo's home as they referred to it, existed as a living personality. As children, they would explore it, discovering secrets in dark corners and secluded rooms.

The house was larger than it appeared on the outside. Its levels were separated by "stairs upon stairs" as Silvya recalled. Toward the front of the home, there was a large, dark and formal parlor room. It had heavy wooden furniture upholstered in deep red velvet and accented with an expectation that children were not permitted to amble around it. The parlor room, like some of the home's other spaces, was designated for adults and their tea, coffee, and whiskey moments.

The kitchen was located past the parlor room, toward the back of the house. As this was the domain of the family's help—the women who prepared their food, maintained their home, and helped raise their kids—few family members spent much time there. Nonetheless, when reflecting on their childhood, Silvya and her cousins' stories quickly shifted to the dishes created in this room. There were soups, such as *sopa de chairo*, a staple of the Bolivian highlands, brimming with *chuños*, a local delicacy made of dehydrated and cheese-soaked potatoes. There were *asados*, or grilled meats, which were prepared over the kitchen's wood burning stove. There was coffee, freshly roasted and ground in a clay pot in the backyard, just a few steps from the kitchen. Always at the end of each meal, there were seasonal fruits for dessert. These included an abundant supply of *chirimoya*. Creamy and sticky-sweet, this fruit became the source of infinite cravings for Silvya as it has been for many Bolivians who have left their country.

Crisologo collected much of his family's produce fresh from the *finca*. Aromas from these foods conjured images of its forest origin. These smells of humidity and soil soaked permanently into the walls and floorboards of his home, just as they did into the lives of the people who spent time there.

Beyond the kitchen, there was a closet-like space. Dark and windowless, the family sometimes used it to store food—those same potatoes, fruits, coca leaves and coffee beans that were grown on the *finca* and then planted in their memories. More often, the family boarded a *cholita* in this space. This woman was responsible for doing most of the family's domestic chores. When they required assistance, needed something to eat, a coffee or tea to drink, or someone to clean up a mess, family members would ring a small bell to summons their *cholita*.

Crisologo's family was not distinguished by having such a room in their home, or by their reliance on a *cholita's* services. Similar realities existed in the residences of most Bolivian families of predominantly European descent. Affording this form of servitude reflected a family's upper crust status, or its attempt to portray this. In many Bolivian homes, as it was in Crisologo's, this did not reflect a conscious cruelty, but rather how things were done, and how they had always been.

Crisologo's home featured other particularities, including a solarium perched at the very top. This room's many windows provided expansive views of the city. This was Crisologo's domain, a place reserved almost exclusively for his benefit. It was his office, napping space, and favored spot for pondering. He spent much of his time up there managing his farm, organizing his affairs, and reflecting on his world.

This space was also particularly hard to reach. Access to it was made possible exclusively via a tightly curved iron staircase. The room's inaccessibility was illustrated when, at age eighty-five and while sitting in his chair, Crisologo died of a heart attack. Following local custom, for one day after his death, his body lay in the room in repose. Perhaps his spirit wanted to spend a little more time taking in the views of La Paz. Whatever the reason, following his wake, his remains stiffened, and became virtually unmovable. The coroner and his crew labored to maneuver the body out of the solarium, down the spiral staircase, through labyrinthine hallways, and eventually to an escape through the front door.

Silvya's father, Humbertó del Rosario Torres Ortíz, was born in October 1902. He was the second of six children. His father, Secundino Torres, was a prominent attorney. His mother, Filomena Ortíz, was a homemaker as well as twenty-two years younger than her husband. His godfather, Ismael Montes, played a significant role in local politics. He was twice elected president of the republic, in 1904 and again in 1913. (Ismael Montes plays a small but notable role in this book which we'll touch on shortly.)

Like the people who surrounded him during his earliest years, Humbertó developed uncommon leadership skills. He was serious but not stern, balancing an outwardly contemplative nature with kindness—this is the first characteristic Silvya offered when asked to describe him.

Results from recent over-the-counter DNA tests prove Silvya's family, like most well-established Latin Americans, can attribute a large percentage of their ancestry to the native peoples who populated the Andes for thousands of years before the European conquest. Reasoning grounded in basic family-tree-investigations suggests Humbertó possessed a substantive portion of these native South American genes. This detail is notable because, until recently, the family has never associated itself with this indigenous heritage. It is possible, even likely, Humbertó and the generations before him did not think of themselves this way. It's either that they did not know their background, or that they did not desire to share it with others.

Humbertó also demonstrated psychic acumen; not the pedestrian type, but evidence of a more pronounced talent. Starting as a child, he could commune with spirits. These spirits were said to move chairs or tables in his presence. They were also known to pick up a pen and write him letters. Both circumstances were validated by witnesses.

As with topics related to his family's native ancestry, Humbertó did not discuss his extra-sense capabilities with many others. These were private attributes; the type we're often encouraged to brush aside or dissect with logic. Not much more is known about this. Yet still today, Silvya along with other family members accept this detail as factual. It seems a description of Humbertó would be incomplete without at least one reference to this skill.

HUMBERTÓ, WITH HIS mixed ancestry and remarkable personality, was a Sureño. That is, he came from Sucre, the capital of the Bolivian department of Chuquisaca. Going back to the European colonization—way back to when Francisco Pizarro engaged the

Inca Empire, back when Sucre was known as Ciudad de la Plata de la Nueva Toledo, or City of Silver of the New Toledo, and for almost four hundred years—Sucre was among the most important settlements in the Americas. Bolivia's and the region's fortunes aligned with the value of the minerals extracted from nearby mines. The country's attention shifted to La Paz only after these resources began to fade.

This historic town of revolutionaries was a fitting backdrop for Humbertó's childhood. As home to the country's judicial branch, and as seat of the Roman Catholic Church in Bolivia, Sucre remains the country's official capital. It is also one of seven locations in Bolivia selected by the United Nations Educational, Scientific, and Cultural Organization (UNESCO) for its cultural, historical, or scientific significance.

The city's history reflects the revolutionary spirit established by Bolivia's namesake and first president, Simón Bolívar. This is where in 1809, from a bell on top of the Basilica de San Francisco, the first *grito libertario*—cry for freedom—was made from any of Spain's colonies in the New World. A few years later, in 1825, Bolivians officially sealed their break from Spanish rule in Sucre in a place now known as *La Casa de la Libertad*—the House of Freedom.

Sucre is home to the Metropolitan Cathedral, which dates to 1559, and the University of Saint-Francois-Xavier Sucre. Founded in 1624, this is among the oldest universities in the New World. The city's architecture reflects its rich history by blending local styles with European influence. Like the experience provided by a visit to *calle* Jaen in La Paz, but on a much grander scale, a visit to Sucre presents an opportunity to step back in time. There are narrow streets paved with cobblestone and lined with white-washed adobe buildings crowned with red clay-tiled roofs. The homes, convents,

churches, schools and government buildings are guarded by
thick weather-worn wooden
doors. Like magical portals,
these doors conceal grand
patios. These are often bursting
with flowering plants—*kantu-
tas*, *patujus*, and *bougainvillea*,
as well as roses, and hydrangea.
The plants are accompanied by
the sounds and sights of songbirds that have emigrated to
Sucre from the nearby tropics.

Façcade in Sucre, 1997

◆ ◆ ◆

HUMBERTÓ'S FATHER PASSED away in 1914. Five years later, his
mother contracted a fatal case of malaria. The evening before she
passed, Humbertó's mother called him to her bedside and challenged him to accomplish something meaningful with his life.
Within a few weeks of her passing, he moved from Sucre to La Paz
to enroll as a cadet in the Bolivian Military Academy.

The academy was first established in Sucre in 1825 by Simón
Bolívar. Over the years, its location has shifted between Sucre and
La Paz. Today, as it was when Humbertó was a cadet, it is situated
in the town of Irpavi, in the basin of the valley that defines the city
of La Paz, not far from the Valley of the Moon, and close to the
Choqueyapu river. Just as the arid riverbed conceals water beneath
it, the academy's nondescript brick exterior hides a world of significance within. For the cadets enrolled there, it is a fortress built

on rules and hierarchy. The academy also represents opportunities that many of these young men might otherwise not have access to. Those who learn to master this environment go on to hold prominent positions within the military and across all aspects of the country's elite class.

Humbertó excelled at the academy. Beyond his academic successes, he displayed considerable aptitude in the extracurricular activities required of blossoming military officers of his era. Cavalry exercises were among his strengths. He enjoyed long rides into the depths of the valley landscape that surrounded him. Venturing well beyond the reach of the city, and farther still approaching the base of Mt. Illimani where cliffs loomed over the riding trails, and water slicing through the ground revealed a rainbow-colored horde of minerals—yellow-tinted rows of sulfur, grey stripes of zinc, and red ribbons of oxidized iron—Humbertó felt free.

His parents' passing led Humbertó to the academy. Sentiments of loyalty and purpose encouraged him to embrace the military as the centerpiece of his life. The practical skills he acquired in the military were enhanced by the many friendships he formed as a cadet and later as an officer. These people, and the camaraderie he shared with them, played a major role in influencing his life.

CHAPTER 4

Lake Titicaca

*Moon rise over Lake Titicaca from Isla del Sol
with Isla de la Luna in the background, 2011*

"Moonrise and sunset on the edge of the clearest sky,
Horizon marked by snowcapped mountains,
Nightfall.
Gaze deeply into the cosmos,
The Milky Way and beyond,
All of this on full display,
Everything,
Accentuated by a rare and pure silence."

—REFLECTIONS FROM LAKE TITICACA,
PERSONAL JOURNAL ENTRY, 1996

I N 1926, HUMBERTÓ graduated as a second lieutenant from the Bolivian Military Academy. For the next three years, he served as an officer in military bases around the Altiplano. These included Puerto Pérez at the base of the Cordillera Real, Oruro a mining town located between La Paz and Sucre, and Puerto Acosta on the shores of Lake Titicaca.

In 1928, while on leave from his post at Puerto Acosta, he met Alicia. They were both vacationing in the town of Copacabana, a popular retreat on Lake Titicaca. One evening, they happened to be on a moonlight tour of the lake. At the end of the tour, Humbertó helped Alicia to shore. Assisted by his lantern, he guided her through the rocks and other obstacles on their path. As she would later describe, he also used the lantern to showcase the silhouette of her figure. Bothered but not offended, she accepted his invitation for a second date when he next visited La Paz.

One year later, Humbertó and Alicia were married in a simple ceremony in La Paz. "My parents had a wonderful relationship, filled with love and respect, until they both died," Silvya said.

IT IS EASY to imagine Lake Titicaca as a romantic retreat. The lake's early inhabitants may have been inspired by this same feeling. As it has always been, the area surrounding it is largely unpopulated. Like the Mediterranean, this environment is arid and sunny. Like a sea, the lake is expansive, covering 3,232 square miles and stretching 118 miles long and fifty miles wide.

Who are we? Why are we? Where are we?

The ancient inhabitants took advantage of the ample open sky to make sense of their world, pursuing questions that are foundational to humanity. They observed the fundamentals—the passage of night and day, the arrival and departure of seasons. They studied the complex—the moon, the planets, the stars, and the patterns these objects created as they crossed the sky over the course of years and decades and centuries. Generations of study led to inspired conclusions. These were articulated in stories and structures. As their language was not captured in written form, much of this narrative has been lost. Many of their buildings have been destroyed or looted to extract their treasures. A few monuments and markers still stand. Isla del Sol, Isla de la Luna, and Tiwanaku provide examples.

The Titikala, which is also known as the Sacred Rock, is a large stone bluff located in an isolated corner on the secluded north-end of Isla del Sol. Unguided, this feature could easily be overlooked. With a touch of assistance, you observe it is shaped like a puma. Indeed, the word *titi* in Quechua and Aymara means puma. Completing the puzzle, the word *caca* means rock. The combination forms the words *Titicaca* or *Titikala* can be interpreted to mean, "rock of the puma."

The Titikala outcrop is also fundamental to the history of local faiths, and to the heritage of the people who have lived in this corner of the world for thousands of years. According to the Inca—the most well-known of the lake's earlier inhabitants, a culture that reigned for a relatively short period of time, and one that drew many of its ideas and customs from its predecessors—the sun's first steps into the sky were aided by indentations, or small steps, chiseled by nature into the face of this rock. From this same spot, *Manco Cápac*, the first man, and his sister-wife, *Mama Ocllo*, followed a similar path.

Unassuming and unadorned—there are no gift shops, and no requests for admission fees—this experience is accessible by foot or boat. Cars are not permitted on the island. A hike from the island's southern tip at Comunidad Yumani, one of its larger villages, to the Titikala is recommended. During the trek, slow down and ease back into another era. Take in the expansive views of the lake and the surrounding mountains of the Cordillera Real. Observe the fields of quinoa, potatoes, and corn—all native Andean crops—as if they were preserved from times past.

Isla de la Luna, is easily accessible from Copacabana, and is even more remote and less touristic than Isla del Sol. There are no stores, restaurants, or hotels on Isla de la Luna; just a few shadowy reflections of its significant past. According to local mythology, this is where the mother moon, when commanded by *Viracocha,* the great creator, took her first steps into the sky.

Today, the reconstructed ruins of the *Iñaq Uyu* remain. This is thought to have been a convent for woman of the noble caste of the Incas. Some of these women were selected for sacrifice. They were brought by raft to the Titikala, and then offered to the universe.

MOVING FURTHER BACK in time, well before the era of the Inca, we arrive at Tiwanaku. This is *the name given* to a culture as well as an archeological site located in Bolivia near Lake Titicaca. *The name given*— because the original name was lost by time.

The Tiwanaku archeological site is another of Bolivia's UNE-SCO World Heritage Sites. While it is now situated eight hundred feet above the surface level of the lake, most archeologists agree, this was once a vibrant port. It is also recognized as one of the most important vestiges of pre-Incan civilization.

The curiosity that surrounds Tiwanaku is enhanced by the architecture and sculpture that exist there. These are purposefully and artistically crafted attempts to express the inexpressible. There are massive structures built from colossal stones. Cut to perfection by the hands of people who possessed a level of skill and precision lost to humankind since the time when they were forged, the stones were then placed in perfect order to create great monuments, plazas, and figures. Rock placed on rock, without requiring any mortar, these structures have withstood environmental conditions and earthquakes well beyond the limits of modern engineering.

There is the *Kalasasaya*, a plaza-temple sunk into the earth. The temple's walls are lined with sculpted faces. These provide a

Kalasasaya temple, Tiwanaku, 2011

glimpse into characteristics that helped define the people of their era. They display a diversity of expressions—joy and sadness, anger and contempt. Surrounded by these sacred idols, you begin to contemplate the significance of Tiwanaku. Some people have suggested these sculptures, their artistry and the overall sophistication exemplified by structures throughout Tiwanaku, reflect intervention from some mysterious and advanced creature—perhaps even an alien lifeform. *How else could the primitive indigenous peoples have achieved such magnificence?*

Similar questions surround archeological sites across the Andes, throughout the Americas, and in ancient places around the world. *Could the same alien creatures have visited all these places? Could they have intervened to help guide human evolution?*

These suppositions diminish human ingenuity and downgrade the quality of thought displayed by earlier generations. While the history surrounding places like Tiwanaku has gaps, all science points to native sources of genius.

THE GATEWAY TO the Sun is among Tiwanaku's most famous archeological features. Ten feet tall, and thirteen feet wide, this massive, solid stone slab dates to around 200 BC. It is adorned with etchings. The main figure reflects the sun god, or perhaps the god of thunder, or maybe the Viracocha—the creator deity. This and other imagery combined with the monument's arched shape suggest it had a ceremonial purpose. It once may have been a lens to help interpret the sky.

Cracked, moved, and reconstructed in the spot in which it was found, this grand archway—originally engineered from a single, enormous slab of stone—may have lost some of its precision. Despite the lost knowledge of its intended purpose, even those who are

Gateway to the Sun, detail, 2011

firmly rooted in their version of the *truth* would struggle to escape the attraction and mystery that surrounds it. Upon the summer and winter solstice, people continue to gather around the Gateway to pay homage to our closest star as its rays pass through its portal.

These sites, Isla del Sol, Isla de la Luna, and Tiwanaku, were recorded in our written history by the Spanish conquistadores. In search of treasure, they came upon these ruins and the articles protected inside them which had been left behind by a vibrant civilization. The Europeans stayed, and committed to convert the indigenous peoples, the descendants of the Tiwanaku, to Christianity. These conquistadores looted shrines for their precious belongings. They deconstructed buildings, prizing their perfectly angular stones for the foundations and walls of their cathedrals and basilicas.

All things go.

IN THE TOWNS and villages surrounding the lake, you will find many examples of colonial era Christian shrines and churches. These remain as monuments to European conquest and conversion. Copacabana, on the shores of Lake Titicaca, provides examples of this heritage, including a sixteenth century basilica dedicated to *Nuestra Señora de Copacabana*—Our Lady of Copacabana—the patron saint of Bolivia. Pilgrims and tourists flock to the basilica to witness its treasure, a wooden effigy of the virgin saint. They also travel to Copacabana as a launching point for visits to the Isla del Sol and Isla de la Luna.

Comunidad Yumani on the Isla del Sol is a short motorboat ride from Copacabana. Alternatively, you can hire a rowboat with a

Basílica de Nuestra Señora de Copacabana, 2011

captain to take you to the island. Embarking from Copacabana, the two-hour journey is appropriately slow and memorable.

Despite increasing tourism, Lake Titicaca and its environs maintains its pristine beauty. A strange spirituality seems to hover around the lake. You can feel it. You can almost see it, radiant blue in form.

CHAPTER 5
The Saltpeter War

Sunset over the Litoral coast, 1996

*"Judgment comes from experience, and
experience comes from bad judgment."*

—SIMÓN BOLÍVAR

Duty, honor, and loyalty—Humbertó espoused these principles. As armies around the world have done for centuries, the Bolivian military programmed him and his fellow soldiers to believe these words reflected a universal human code. Men who aspired to become professional officers of competence and character were required to adhere to it.

Class-based hierarchy, allegiance without question, and racial favoritism—as Humbertó began his career, some of the other beliefs present in his corner of Bolivian society were becoming increasingly unsuitable for the majority of the country's citizens. Indigenous Bolivians were less inclined to be subjugated to the rules imposed on them by a Europeanized elite minority. Politicians and military leaders—often the same individuals—were reluctant to recognize this.

Relative to many, Humbertó was progressive in his leadership style, and in his beliefs regarding how his country should be run. Always looking beyond his escalating rank and status, he never condescended or attempted to talk down to anyone. He was a collaborative team member, and a skilled negotiator. Instinctively, he understood the essential obligation to separate Bolivia's military and political interests.

Forward leaning and influential as he was, as an individual, Humbertó was incapable of redirecting the course of a nation firmly rooted in antiquated rules and structures. To understand his circumstance and the events that defined modern Bolivia, it is essential to review the country's major conflicts. The South American War of the Pacific, also known as the Saltpeter War, is perhaps the most significant of these conflicts. The war took place between 1879 and 1883 in what was then Bolivia's Litoral Department, the coastal expanse adjacent to the Atacama Desert, and allied Bolivia with Peru against Chile.

ENCIRCLED BY THE Peruvian Andes, the Chilean Costal Range, the Bolivian Altiplano, and the Pacific Ocean, the Atacama Desert holds the distinction as the world's driest place outside of Antarctica. The desert's proximity to the South American highlands combined with strong winds coming off the Pacific Ocean ensures moisture is extremely rare. The Atacama receives less than one millimeter of rain annually, a depth approximating the thickness of a fingernail.

The arid environment appears extraterrestrial and lifeless. Yet somehow it supports a diversity of organisms, from algae, to flamingos and vicuñas. Hot during the day, and cold at night, the desert is alive with sounds of crackling earth, singing birds, and whistling wind. The landscape is marked with ancient volcanoes and expansive salt flats. These are the tombstones of vanished seas. The Atacama is not just one of the world's driest deserts, it is also among the oldest.

This desert connects Bolivia with its neighbors, Chile and Peru. All barriers separating these countries are merely political, conjured in relatively recent times. Regardless of their citizenship, the stout and acclimatized indigenous people who inhabit the Atacama are genetically and culturally similar. They survive through ingenuity. They build homes from earthen blocks and volcanic rocks. They guide water from the mountains to their terraced fields. They raise llamas and alpacas for meat and wool. They have lived this way since before recorded time.

Their ancestors' burial grounds, or *chullpas*, dot the landscape and testify to the society's longevity. Undisturbed by water or outsiders, these earthen structures can preserve their contents for centuries. It is possible, even easy, to find mummified bodies in these *chullpas* just as people placed them hundreds of years before—curled up, knees-to-chest, and adorned with textiles and tools intended to help guide the deceased in the afterlife.

FROM THE ATACAMA, to the Altiplano, and the Amazon basin, Bolivia's geological and biological variety position it in the top tier of the world's most diverse countries. Conversely, the country's military history is largely unvarying, and defined by a steady series of coup d'états and wartime defeats.

During the South American War of the Pacific, Hilarión Daza Groselle was Bolivia's president. A career military officer, he came to power in a coup orchestrated against his predecessor, Tomás Frías. Under Frías, Bolivia and Chile had signed a treaty stipulating Bolivia would not increase taxes on Chilean-owned businesses or Chilean citizens operating in the Litoral. The treaty made sense. Much of the infrastructure in the Litoral as well as most of its residents were Chilean. Even so, the new Bolivian leadership, under President Daza Groselle, struggled with the terms of this treaty, believing it undermined the country's sovereignty, as well as its prospects for increased tax revenue. In 1878, Bolivia broke the treaty by imposing a new tax on Chilean mining operations.

The disagreement focused on the substance that gave the conflict its name. Mineral exports from the Litoral represented a major portion of the Andean region's total economy. These minerals included saltpeter, also known as potash, potassium nitrate, or simply nitrate. From fertilizers to gunpowder, this substance was a primary ingredient in a wide range of industrial and military products. It was extracted from the ample sources of bird *guano* existing along the Pacific coast. (The word *guano* originated from Quechua, the language of the Inca.) It is accurate to conclude that this South American War of the Pacific, the Saltpeter War, an event that resulted in the death of more than twenty thousand people, had its origins in excrement.

For Bolivia, the war was a complete catastrophe and became a nationalist battle cry for the next century. The country lost its coastline, ceding the Pacific ports of Tocopilla, Mejillones, and Antofagasta to Chile. This loss fundamentally altered Bolivia's geography and economy, as well as the psychology of its people. Living separated from the Pacific Ocean by distances of as little as seventy-five miles, generations of Bolivians have never known the ocean, its power and expanse.

Today, Bolivia maintains a navy, but its role is mostly symbolic. A small fleet of undersized boats patrols Lake Titicaca and rivers throughout the country. Even so, the Bolivian military continues to hold onto an antiquated mantra which sums up the sentiment of many of its citizens: *Lo que un día fue nuestro, nuestro otra vez será.* What was once ours, will be ours again.

BOLIVIANS BLAMED LOSING the war on uncommitted and greedy politicians and a poorly funded and insufficiently prepared military. Following the war, President Daza Groselle, a focal point for culpability, fled to Europe. He lived there in exile for the next fourteen years. In 1894, enticed by what he perceived as an opportunity to clear his name, he returned to Bolivia. Shortly after entering the country, in the Uyuni train station at the edge of the Atacama Desert, he was assassinated.

The last decade of the nineteenth century initiated a new era for Bolivia. While the developed world, led by North America, Europe and Japan, began to progress toward industrialization, Bolivia regrouped, and experimented with its own take on modernizing its military, politics, and economy.

Committed to forming a more professional armed force, a fresh round of Bolivian leaders got to work. They reorganized the military into zones which were roughly aligned with the country's geography and departmental structure. They increased investment in the military. They removed older officers from their posts and replaced them with younger ones. In 1891, they reopened the Bolivian Military Academy, which had been closed since 1847, and moved it from Sucre to its current location in Irpavi just outside of La Paz.

The nation's leaders also looked abroad, to Europe and the US, for guidance. Whereas in the past politicians and military officials had controlled Bolivia's mines, businessmen now stepped in to manage the country's vast natural resources. Foreign investors joined with local leaders to capitalize on spiking demand for raw materials. These Bolivian leaders included the most famous of the nation's industrialists, Simón Patiño. Born near Cochabamba, Bolivia and referred to as the Andean Rockefeller, at the time of his death in 1947, Patiño had become one of the wealthiest people in the world.

Patiño's wealth came from tin. This soft and pliable metal existed in abundance in Bolivia. For centuries, miners discarded it as refuse due to its lower-tier commercial value. In the last decades of the nineteenth century, as the global industrial engine ignited, demand for tin spiked. Suddenly, it became a critical component of an expanding array of manufacturing processes. The fabrication of food cans, windowpanes, and electrical wires all required it.

By the beginning of the twentieth century, tin mining emerged as a primary contributor to the Bolivian economy. From 1900 to 1910, domestic production increased from twelve to twenty percent of the world's supply. By the 1920s, tin represented seventy percent of the total value of Bolivian exports. (Contreras 1993, 3)

Politicians and generals aspired to learn from their country's previous mistakes and direct a prosperous, new course for Bolivia. Their reforms and investments, though, did little to temper the aspirations and greed of leading members of their society. Feeding an insatiable demand for raw materials, industrialists searched beyond silver and tin for new sources to help fuel economic expansion. They looked inward, continuing to exploit Bolivian resources. They also looked to their neighbors.

◆ ◆ ◆

In 1904, TWENTY years after hostilities had ceased, Bolivia's president and Humbertó's godfather, Ismael Montes, signed a definitive peace treaty with Chile. Under President Montes, Bolivia begrudgingly accepted the loss of its former territories in exchange for a Chilean-funded railway linking La Paz with the nearby coastal town of Arica. In spirit, Bolivians reacquired some access to the sea.

The focus of Bolivian aspirations shifted from the Pacific Ocean to the Chaco Boreal, a hot and sparsely populated expanse spread along Bolivia's border with Brazil and Paraguay. Oil barons from Bolivia and abroad suspected the Chaco held vast fuel reserves. In the earlier years of South American history, the Chaco was combined with the Litoral Department and Bolivia's current territorial boundaries to form a single Spanish colonial district. Expansionist-minded Bolivians inferred these earlier boundaries were set in perpetuity. The Chaco, and all that it contained, was rightfully and permanently theirs.

Beyond antiquated territorial claims and potential mineral wealth, the Chaco held practical benefits. The great Río Paraguay crosses the region on its meandering path to the Río de la Plata, which connects to the Atlantic Ocean. Securing this territory would have provided Bolivia with much-desired port access. Aging politicians and military relics from the Saltpeter War, along with a new breed of nationalist-leaning Bolivians, longed for this. Despite their treaties with Chile, in their hearts, they never let go of the concept of a greater Bolivia with free and open access to the sea.

THE CHACO WAR lasted from June 1932 to June 1935. While unknown to most people outside of South America, it was the deadliest war in all the Americas in the last century. At the outset, both sides faced daunting logistics. Swamps, excessive heat, vast distances and horrible infrastructure obstructed the movement of troops and supplies.

Looking past these obstacles, Bolivian leaders concluded this would be an easy win. Bolivia had three million citizens, and Paraguay had less than one million. Bolivia's military was much larger and more technologically advanced than Paraguay's. Also, Bolivia had a much larger, more diverse economy than its adversary.

Despite these numerous advantages, Bolivia's leaders miscalculated the sentiments of most of the country's citizens who viewed the Chaco as a distant land with limited cultural connection to the rest of the nation. The rank and file soldiers certainly did not want to get injured or die fighting to secure this unknown and undesirable territory.

Whereas Bolivia approached the conflict overconfidently, Paraguay viewed it as a must-win circumstance. Since liberation from Spain, Paraguay had lost much of its territory to Argentina, Brazil, and Uruguay. Rendered landlocked like Bolivia, and with a large portion of its remaining land residing in the Chaco, Paraguay could not afford to lose any more of its resources.

In the end, neither Bolivia nor Paraguay received much of anything for their sacrifices. The Chaco's supposed expansive oil reserves turned out to be fable. For Bolivia, the war was a particularly costly disaster. While there is no precise calculation of the number of casualties suffered during the war, between 50,000 and 65,000 Bolivians—approximately 2 percent of the country's total population—are estimated to have died in the conflict. Bolivia lost more territory to Paraguay than Paraguay had even claimed at the start of the conflict. The notion Bolivia had entered the war with a better equipped and trained army proved false. The nation's failures aggravated a sense of frustration among its younger veterans, including Humbertó. This group became known as the Chaco Generation. Charging that collusion between Bolivian politicians and international oil companies had led Bolivia into another disastrous war, the veterans—as their predecessors had done at the end of the Saltpeter War—began to challenge the established political system.

CHAPTER 6

The War of
the Thirst

Where the jungle ends, Chaco, Bolivia, 1997

*"The history of Bolivia from its independence is nothing
other than the repetition, if not the succession of the
same political, economic, diplomatic, and military
events, with so many or greater deficiencies each time."*

—CAPITAN HUMBERTÓ TORRES ORTÍZ, 1937

S ILVYA'S ASSESSMENT OF the Chaco War formed out of her
parents' views. "I was not alive during the conflict, and I don't
remember studying it in school," she said. "Either it wasn't a topic,
or I just didn't care to pay attention when it was taught. My parents
didn't discuss it much either, but there were a few stories, and of
course, there is my father's book."

This book, *Campo Vía* (Ortíz 1937), is a memoir and exploration
into the political circumstances surrounding the war, as well as the
military tactics used in it. Humbertó described foreign intervention
and influence as a main contributor to Bolivia's failures in the war.
Hans Kundt, a German national and military officer, personified
this influence. In 1908, the Bolivian government, headed by President Ismael Montes, hired Kundt to reorganize its military in the
image of the Prussian Army. At the start of the Frist World War,
Kundt returned to Europe to command a German regiment on the
Eastern Front. Following the war, he went back to Bolivia where he

served as the chief of staff of the army, and then Bolivia's minister of war. In 1930, he was exiled from the country for participating in a coup against Bolivia's president, Hernando Siles Reyes. Two years later, a new president, Daniel Salamanca Urey, invited Kundt back to serve as commander in chief, the head of the Bolivian military, and charged him with leading the nation against Paraguay.

According to Humbertó, despite Kundt's cocksure assessment of Bolivia's aptitude and appetite for war, he underutilized the officers under his command. He assigned men to positions that did not allow them to function beyond the small circles they were placed in. Humbertó summarized Kundt's impact, "when the head is bad, the feet walk worse."

HUMBERTÓ BELIEVED PARAGUAYANS wanted war. Their leaders understood their advantages including their familiarity with the Chaco—from its unforgiving climate to its lethal snakes and insects. They did not discriminate when recruiting soldiers—their ages ranged from fourteen to fifty years old. Enhancing their advantage, Paraguayans deployed unconventional military tactics, managing to outwit the Bolivians by entangling them, damaging them, and then fleeing the battleground. Bolivians, seeped in outdated military techniques, were ill-prepared. As Humbertó described, "these men were most comfortably placed in the Altiplano."

Despite Paraguay's advantages, Humbertó believed the war could have been decided in Bolivia's favor had its citizens rallied for the cause. If the government, the army, and the people had shared the will, "the enemy from the southeast... small and poor Paraguay," could not have conjured the resources required to sustain a campaign of any duration. Bolivian leaders, and Hans Kundt in particular, made a ruinous calculation. They believed the war would only last a few months. Humbertó wrote, "Our country was taken in diapers. As ill-prepared as we were, the enemy's propaganda machine convinced the Paraguayan people Bolivia was the second most powerful military in all of South America."

IN BOLIVIA, THIS war has many names—*La Guerra del Campo, La Guerra con Paraguay,* and *La Guerra de la Sed,* or The War of Thirst. Bolivian soldiers relied on equipment, food and water that was transported to them, often by foot, from far away. If logistics lines slowed or were disrupted by the Paraguayan military, Bolivian soldiers suffered. If these disruptions occurred during the rainy season, soldiers could source water from rivers and streams. If the disruptions occurred during the dry season, soldiers, like thirsty animals, scrambled to find the few remaining puddles or mudholes.

Battles were lost, and men died not because the Paraguayan forces outnumbered or outmaneuvered the Bolivians, but due to poor planning. The shortage of potable water was so great the rationing of liquid was limited to one-and-a-half cups per soldier per day.

Humbertó added, "There were days when the total number of available ammunitions for our canons did not reach a score. While the enemy harassed us day and night with its fire, our troops received orders not to shoot due to the scarcity of ammunition."

DURING THE WAR, Humbertó served as a captain of the cavalry in the Bolivian Army's Fourth Division. He was responsible for a battalion of approximately forty men, along with several dozen horses, and a handful of trucks and tanks. Both of Alicia's brothers, Julio and Criso, were assigned to his command.

Each week, Alicia and her sisters, Filomena, Betty, Nena, and Marina, helped their stepmother, Mama Carmen, prepare gifts for the three soldiers. Their packages contained traditional items—letters from loved ones, newspapers, and cigarettes. They also included uniquely Bolivian items—caramels from Sucre, and powdered *api*, a traditional Bolivian breakfast drink fashioned from purple maize, sugar and cinnamon. At the beginning of the war, these gifts traveled by train, truck and horse—one day, perhaps two—from the Altiplano down to their destination in the Paraguayan campo; an eight-hundred-kilometer journey to a place that may have seemed like a world away but was actually quite accessible. As the conflict progressed, deteriorating logistics halted this sort of casual contact between Bolivia's citizens and its soldiers.

COMBAT HIGHLIGHTED THE Bolivian Army's weaknesses. In September 1933, Humbertó fought in the Battle of Campo Grande. The Paraguayan Army encircled two Bolivian regiments forcing hundreds of soldiers to surrender. Humbertó lamented, "these men, defeated by the enemy of thirst, swelled the ranks of captive Bolivians." As the number of available Bolivian men of fighting age declined, the target age for recruits increased from eighteen, to twenty-five, to thirty years old and above.

Three months later, in December 1933, Humbertó fought in the Battle of Campo Vía. He described the location—a *pajonal*, or expansive grassland, surrounded by the great Chaqueña jungle. Humbertó compared the environment to hell. "In this place, nature is man's first enemy, and his most powerful adversary."

No true roads connected the battleground with supply lines; most were just dry riverbeds. At the start of the conflict, vehicles and horses brought soldiers water, food, and armaments from camps located nearby. As these resources became exhausted, the army had to source supplies from much further away. Poor weather and over-use damaged supply routes and immobilized vehicles. Horses were injured on the trails or killed in battle. Soldiers replaced them, carting the supplies on their backs and by foot.

While the Bolivians suffered, Paraguayan forces went on the offensive. "A grenade exploded next to me," Humbertó wrote from Campo Vía. "It dissolved a group of soldiers sitting next to me, leaving nothing left but smoke and dust. Pieces of their bodies dangled from the grass and bushes."

Exhausted and without reinforcements or the prospect of receiving them, the Bolivian Fourth Division was reduced to an assemblage of maimed and lame invalids. Unaware or undisturbed, General Kundt remained obsessed with the notion the enemy countered with an inferior force. He ordered his men to retreat and regroup. Anticipating this maneuver, the Paraguayans surrounded the Bolivians and harassed them with a constant artillery bombardment. One-by-one, Bolivian regiments surrendered. The men that remained were reduced to a delusional state. Those that continued to fight were wiped out.

Pitiless Paraguayan forces or the unforgiving Pachamama filled drinking wells with saltwater. "Soldiers, seized by hunger and thirst, walked in circles as if they were looking for something they'd lost on the ground," Humbertó wrote.

"A group of twelve or so men were huddled on the side of the road next to a carcass of a cow. They must have spotted the animal in a field. It had clearly been neglected. Deprivation had cut its frame down to bone. The cow now lay upside down in a makeshift firepit with its legs in the air and back against the flames. Men stood by waiting for what must have felt like their first meal."

An order came in from Bolivia's top generals, "destroy all equipment and armaments."

Humbertó lamented, "and this is how a cavalry ends."

Two thousand Bolivians died at Campo Vía, and seven thousand more were taken prisoner. As a result, Hans Kundt was relieved of his command. He returned to Germany and died in Switzerland in 1939.

HUMBERTÓ'S BOOK, *CAMPO Vía*, does not include a description of the end of his wartime experience. Silvya's cousin, Fernando, provided some of the missing details. He described, "During the Battle of Campo Vía, my father (Alicia's brother Julio) became very ill. Doctors removed him from the battlefield because they thought he would die. That removal is what saved him. The Paraguayans captured my uncles (Humbertó and Criso) and imprisoned them for a year. They were freed by the amnesty that followed the war."

Silvya added, "I do not remember much about the Chaco War, but I do recall one of my father's stories from Campo Vía. As he was fleeing the Paraguayans, he came across a puddle. He dipped his head to take a drink, and noticed the water was colored red. Looking around him, he saw arms and legs from many soldiers floating in the water or sticking out of the mud. These sorts of experiences discouraged him from talking with me about the war."

HUMBERTÓ SUMMARIZED HIS sentiments. "Revolutions and coups d'état, the disorganization of the intellectual classes and workers, and the exploitation of our main sources of production by foreign elements has manifested in a constant malaise of economic crisis. The lack of success of our diplomacy in maintaining relations with other countries, particularly with our neighbors. The interference of the army in politics, while abandoning or neglecting military preparation. All of this contributed to the near collapse of the nation." He added, "Reviewing the military campaigns since our independence, these have not served our education other than delighting us with a little reading. They are all tales of the same political and military errors. A period of restoration follows the war; time which serves to amend and correct our failures."

After the war, Humbertó and other leaders once again set out to analyze and learn from their failures. They vowed to not fall victim to the same mistakes. They committed to dedicate the proper resources to developing the next generation of soldiers. They would look to outside leadership—the best in the world—to ensure their soldiers received proper training. In the event of war, they would secure the means required to win. Bolivia would guard its borders. The country would be prepared for any attack. But the adversaries and circumstances Humbertó imagined turned out to be false. Bolivia's next conflict came from within the country.

Echoing the country's loss to Paraguay in the Chaco War, miners and other workers across Bolivia began to express discontent. Their unrest partially reflected the country's and its citizens' dimmed fortunes from the global Great Depression. It also represented a sense of general unrest reverberating from the other war unfolding a half-a-world away, in Europe.

From 1930 to 1950, thirteen presidents or military or judicial heads of state served Bolivia. Over this same period, the country's political landscape transformed. New parties were created including the communist-leaning *Partido de la Izquierda Revolucionaria*, or Revolutionary Left Party, the Francisco Franco-inspired *Falange Socialista Boliviana*, or Bolivian Socialist Falange, and what would become the most influential political party of all, the *Movimiento Nacionalista Revolucionario*, the Nationalist Revolutionary Movement, or MNR.

In 1942, Ángel Víctor Paz Estenssoro, an economics professor, and Hernán Siles Zuazo, a political reformist and son of a former Bolivian president, joined labor leaders and intellectuals to create the MNR. Party members pursued egalitarian concepts including extending voting rights to indigenous Bolivians, and reallocating land back to indigenous ownership. Their movement reflected a major shift in Latin American politics, a challenge to the era of elitist rule.

CHAPTER 7

Potosí

Potosí with the Cerro Rico in the background, 1997

> *"...the treasures of Venice, the mines of*
> *Potosí, would be insufficient to pay thee."*

— MIGUEL DE CERVANTES, *DON QUIXOTE*

S ITUATED IN SOUTHWESTERN Bolivia, ninety-seven miles from Sucre or 337 miles from La Paz and hovering in rarified air at an altitude beyond the nosebleed-inducing 13,000-foot mark, Potosí, another UNESCO World Heritage Site, is among the highest cities in the world. While Potosí endures as a hidden gem on the fringes of the adventure tourism circuit, this dusty and isolated, yet colorful spot was once a principal player in world economics.

Founded in 1545, the Villa Imperial de Potosí—as it was designated by Francisco Álvarez de Toledo, the viceroy of Peru—was until the eighteenth century one of the largest cities in the Americas. For a period, its population even exceeded London's. It was home to the *Casa de la Moneda,* The House of Money, the first royal mint of the Spanish empire in the Americas.

Don Quixote referenced Potosí as a land of extraordinary riches. Thanks to Cervantes, the word, Potosí, entered Spanish vernacular where it lives today conjuring images of great wealth and prosperity. Attempting to skim off elements of this fame, towns across the Americas have named themselves in honor of this memorable outpost.

The city's notoriety, and the essence of its wealth, emanates from one colossal rock. The *Cerro Rico*, or Rich Hill, housed mineral deposits of such significance they enabled this otherwise minor geologic feature to play a monumental role in financing the Spanish Golden Era. This period began in 1556 when Felipe II ascended to the throne of Spain and Portugal. For the next century, master writers and painters—Cervantes, Lope de Vega, Diego Velázquez, El Greco, along with many others—produced timeless works of art. Appropriated Bolivian silver, more than gold, and certainly more than human ingenuity, fueled this epoch of creativity, exploration, and cultural renaissance.

Within the *Cerro Rico*, a labyrinth of mining tunnels connects to a web of, what were once, thick and nearly solid veins of silver. These extend from deep beneath the Earth's surface to the tip of the *Cerro Rico* close to 16,000 feet above sea level. Testifying to Spanish imperial opulence, it is fabled enough metal was extracted from this rock to allow for the creation of a road extending from the mine's entrance to the doors of the cathedral in the center of town and cobbled with bricks of pure silver.

By the end of the nineteenth century, depleted silver resources coupled with declining prices prompted industrialists to change their focus. Tin surpassed silver as the most valuable mineral extracted from the *Cerro Rico*. Not long after, when tin resources within the mine became depleted, greedy eyes shifted to the town's monuments and buildings. These structures were made from tin-laden stones taken from the mine. Looters and profiteers dismantled centuries-old homes and churches, many featuring finely crafted facades which were among the most exquisite examples of colonial era stonework in existence in the New World. Their attention shifted away from Potosí only after most of the treasure had been drained from it.

Today, the mines of the *Cerro Rico* are managed as workers' cooperatives. More than before, these workers manage the mines and resources extracted from them to the benefit of the men and women who labor inside them.

Passage into the mines is permissible for miners as well as thrill-seeking tourists. Entrance happens through the many holes that burrow into the mountain like cavities in a rotting tooth. Near the surface, air passes swiftly into these passageways which drives temperatures down to levels approaching freezing. Extending just a few hundred yards deeper into these tunnels, temperatures rise sharply. This abrupt change is caused by something geologists refer to as the geothermal gradient—heat rises with increased proximity to the Earth's molten core.

Each of these tunnels can extend for more than a kilometer. The endpoints are where the pursuit of wealth halts, if only temporarily.

El Tío in the Cerro Rico, 1997

Many of these are guarded by demons—ornate stone sculptures of the devil incarnate, complete with devious smiles, grotesque horns, and erect, oversize penises.

Laughable for outsiders, these statues serve a solemn, even spiritual, purpose. They are referred to by the miners as *El Tío*, or The Uncle. Miners place them deep within the mountain to honor the wealth produced by the innards of our planet. They adorn them with gifts of cigarettes and coca leaves. As added enticement, they offer *El Tío* vials of *alcohol puro*. Two hundred-proof and crystal-clear, this liquid is the same substance as the solvent used around the world to disinfect wounds. In Bolivia, it is also consumed as a potent, albeit impermanent, method to cleanse one's troubles. The *El Tío* statues and the offerings surrounding them symbolize gratitude—for miners' safety, for their jobs, and for the mountain's everlasting abundance.

For five hundred years, the depths of the *Cerro Rico* have fueled armies, dynasties, and entire societies. The minerals extracted from these mines have also helped create the very concept of a global economy. They are the foundation for one of the first instances of commerce between the New and Old Worlds.

El Tío is also a reminder this wealth has come with a cost of extraordinary hardship and great pain. Over the course of these past five centuries, an estimated eight million people—a figure large enough to warrant a repeat—eight million humans have died working the mines of Potosí.

The history of the *Cerro Rico* is one of exploitation—of indigenous Bolivians and African slaves by an elite group of overseer masters. Similar experiences have been replicated across the country, throughout Latin America, and around the world. While this scale of abuse is not unique in our human history, the intensity of suffering surrounding such a specific geological feature is remarkable.

Before these metals were hammered into bricks, before they were pressed and stamped into coins, before they traveled by llama and mule to the Pacific for ongoing transport to the isthmus of Panama, the launching pad for the trans-oceanic journey to Spain, these metals existed undisturbed beneath the earth in this secluded and mysterious corner of the Bolivian Altiplano. The precise mixture of geologic phenomena that make this place so exceptional is almost unprecedented.

All along, miners have continued to labor in the *Cerro Rico*. Periodically, they discover new and untapped pockets of tin, zinc, or even silver. Simultaneously, a tension between these exploited Bolivians and the country's elite grows. At times, tension erupts. Then it subsides, but only for a period before building toward a next release.

CHAPTER 8

Torino

Mt. Blanc and the Alps, 2008

> *"Three cheers for the war. Three cheers for Italy's war and three cheers for war in general. Peace is hence absurd or rather a pause in war."*

—BENITO MUSSOLINI

IN THE YEARS leading up to the Second World War, both Allied and Axis powers identified Latin America as a region ripe with strategic potential. The region contained massive, and still largely untapped, mineral and fuel deposits. These resources held the promise of powering either side through the looming global conflict. For the overhasty individuals who dared to look further into the future, Latin America and its resources promised to be a difference maker after the war as they pursued their nations' long-term aspirations.

Both sides worked to secure alliances with governments throughout Central and South America. Focused on maintaining stable and open access to the Panama Canal, the United States and United Kingdom initially focused on Central America. Germany and Italy concentrated their attention on the Southern Cone countries of Argentina, Chile, Paraguay, and Bolivia. While claiming neutrality, Bolivia invested in cultivating its alliance with the Axis nations.

Bolivia and Germany already shared significant military connections and history. Otto Philipp Braun, from the city of Kassel in present-day Germany, worked as a chief advisor to Simón Bolívar. After South American independence, in 1830, Braun moved to Bolivia where he served as one of the country's most successful generals.

By the 1930s, a sizable German population had settled in Bolivia. These people were part of a wave of European emigration to Latin America. Most of these emigrants selected Argentina and Chile, but many moved to Bolivia. As exemplified by Hans Kundt, this new expat community influenced the country's military and political affairs. The community also helped direct the nation's economic fortunes. German nationals stepped in to control prominent local businesses including the national airline, Lloyd Aéreo Boliviano.

Members of the Bolivian elite became attracted to the Nazi government's technical and military prowess, which had begun to be demonstrated with great effect in Europe. Before the outbreak of war, German military advisors selected a handful of Bolivian officers to move to Italy for specialized training. They identified Humbertó for this duty.

In 1938, he and Alicia, accompanied by then one-year-old Silvya and her six-year-old sister, Gloria, left for Europe. Their voyage began on an ocean liner which embarked from Arica, Chile, a port town on the edge of the Atacama Desert which Chile had gained from Peru during the Saltpeter War. Their boat hugged the edge of the South American Pacific coast, passed through the Panama Canal, and then across the Atlantic toward their new home in Turin, Italy.

While in Italy, Humbertó's military curriculum consisted of leadership courses, history, and field exercises. By orchestrating simulated missions and troop movements in the Italian Alps, he learned offensive and defensive strategies including how to success-fully maneuver a large army through rugged terrain. German and Italian military leaders designed these presumably modern warfare tactics to prepare Humbertó and his fellow officers from across the Southern Cone to defend their countries. Germany and Italy bene-fited from the exportation of their military expertise as well as the evangelization of their cultural, economic, and political ideologies. All of this in anticipation of a future, fascist-controlled world order.

Humbertó was becoming an insider in a new Bolivian govern-ment, with global connections and far-reaching aspirations.

SILVYA RETAINS SOME of the details from her childhood experi-ence in Italy. She remembers the day her brother, Gustavo, who is known as Beto, was born in Turin. She recalls her father's nervous-ness during the hours leading up to his son's birth. She can picture the pride and humility reflected in her father's face the moment he shared the news that she, now and forever, had a brother.

Silvya also remembers her family's apartment—nicely posi-tioned, only steps from Turin's *Piazza Castello*. She remembers the colors of her apartment walls and the city streets: mustard-yellow, brick-red, and cream. She recalls her mother's accounts of the city, and the associations she made between northern Italy and the Andes.

Turin and La Paz both display beautiful samples of baroque architecture—the Basilica of San Francisco in La Paz with its mem-orable baroque-mestizo style; the Church of San Lorenzo in Turin with its notably complex and colorful interior. Like La Paz with its Illimani and the other mountains of the Cordillera Real looming as the backdrop, Turin is positioned at the base of the Italian Alps with many peaks including *Monte Cervino*—the Matterhorn—and Mt. Blanc both visible in the distance.

While living in Italy, Alicia could trick herself to believe she was at home. Daily visits to churches and plazas coupled with visions of mountains and snow made the seemingly infinite distance separating her from La Paz feel surmountable.

Long after returning to Bolivia, Alicia would fondly refer to Turin as an almost-Bolivian city. In turn, she described La Paz as a city with European style and sensibilities. Such a comparison between American and European cities is one of the great compliments New World inhabitants can bestow upon the places they love.

As the family settled into their European lifestyle, Italy and Germany became increasingly preoccupied with their escalating wartime commitments. These governments temporarily set aside dreams and aspirations of physical and ideological expansions in South America. Their attention shifted to attempting to secure newly conquered European and African possessions.

In June 1940, Benito Mussolini declared war on France and England. Within twenty-four hours, Royal Air Force planes began to bomb Italy. Due to its location and economic significance as a leading manufacturing center, Turin was the first city targeted by these raids. In addition to slowing industrial production, the Allies' goal was to provoke fear and anxiety among the general population. Allied bombing was intended to persuade Italians, if not their government, to withdraw support for Mussolini and his fascist regime.

"As I was just a few years old, I'm not sure which of my thoughts are true memories or just bad dreams," Silvya said. "As the bombing began, everyone had to go down to the basement in our apartment building. I remember going up and down the stairs, sometimes several times in one day. After the bombing ended, the sirens returned, telling us we could go back home. All of this was very hard for my mother with her three children."

As the war progressed, the Axis governments viewed Humbertó's and his cohorts' mission in Italy as an afterthought. Even so, their training regimen continued for two more years. In October 1942, Humbertó and his family returned to Bolivia. Their departure coincided with a high mark in the trajectory of Mussolini's *Partito Nazionale Fascista*, the Italian National Fascist Party. Weeks later, Axis control of the African front collapsed. This exposed Italy to an invasion by Allied forces, which commenced one year later. In the interim, Allied bombing of Italian cities continued. Bombing, combined with a lack of food and fuel, demoralized the population.

FOR SILVYA AND her siblings, memories of the war lingered after they returned to Bolivia. She said, "during the day, we were normal children, except we preferred to speak Italian. At night, things were different. I had nightmares. I would wake up pulling my hair. I went to a doctor. He heard me speaking Italian, which led him to ask more questions. He learned where we had been living, what my father had been doing, and some of the things we had experienced."

The doctor's conclusion: Silvya suffered from the condition referred to today as post-traumatic stress disorder. Her recollection of wartime images and sounds, a minor echo of the experiences felt by millions of people from around the world, lingered. Even today, at the other end of her long life, Silvya remembers. She recalls the apartment cellar, not all the details, but the feeling—dark and musty, yet warm and safe. She can feel the impact of bombs blasting on the streets above her family's home. She can see her mother's, sister's, and brother's candlelit faces as they huddled together. She can hear her mother's voice: "It's okay. Stay quiet my love. All of this will be over soon."

CHAPTER 9

Prelude to a Revolution

Street laborer in La Paz, 2011

> *"Bolivia is a majority indigenous nation, but that majority has always been excluded."*

—EVO MORALES

AFTER RETURNING FROM Italy, Humbertó and his family moved to Cochabamba. This city is located 230 miles east of La Paz, at the foot of the 16,500-foot Mt. Tunari and on the eastern-most edge of the Andes range. Cochabamba's 8,000-foot elevation is relaxing by Bolivian standards. Its name, Cochabamba, is derived from the Quechua words *khocha* and *pampa*, meaning "a plain with many lakes." Reflecting this heritage, Bolivians refer to it as the "Garden City." This phrase accurately reflects the favorable climate but establishes false expectations for this often brown and dusty environment.

Lush vegetation begins outside the city, in the adjacent Chapare province. Like the Yungas near La Paz, the Chapare is a cloud forest-gateway to the South American lowlands. It is also the hub of Bolivian cocaine production and trafficking. Proximity to these activities and the characters involved in them has tainted the city's reputation. From the 1970s to the 1990s, men like Roberto Suárez Gómez, the King of Cocaine, established Cochabamba and the adjacent jungle as a major point in the South

American cocaine supply chain. Suárez inspired the character Alejandro Sosa, the Cochabamba-based drug lord, in the 1983 film *Scarface*. Bolivian police arrested Suárez in 1988 and sentenced him to fifteen years in prison in La Paz. He died in 2000 and is buried near Cochabamba.

Drawing a distinction from its reputation for criminal dealings, Cochabamba is also celebrated for its history as well as its monuments. It was the site of a precursor to colonial rebellion on the South American continent—a women-led riot against the Spanish Army which occurred on May 27, 1812. In remembrance of that event, Bolivians now mark May 27th as Mother's Day. The Cristo de la Concordia, the Christ of Peace, one of the largest statues of Jesus in the world, stands watch over the city. This effigy reminds Cochabamba's visitors of the city's and country's Catholic heritage and values. Its outstretched arms suggest reverent supervision over the people who live there.

THE ARMY PROMOTED Humbertó to colonel and assigned him to the post of commander of the *Escuela de Aplicación de Armas*. This newly created post-graduate military school, which was in Cochabamba, reflected the government's strengthened commitment to ensuring military preparation.

As commander, Humbertó had an opportunity to showcase his advanced leadership skills and wartime experience. His position enabled him to guide young soldiers who, like him only a handful of years before, had arrived at the academy to transform themselves into military men. Across his career, educating and mentoring soldiers was the duty Humbertó most enjoyed.

Humbertó and the officers under his command set out to prepare the soldiers. Their curriculum included training missions in the mountains and jungles surrounding Cochabamba. Substituting the Andes for the Alps, Humbertó utilized the military strategies and tactics he learned in Italy. Thanks in part to his leadership, more than ever before, the army was ready to defend the nation against any future invasion.

WHILE LIVING IN Cochabamba, Silvya attended a Catholic school. This education was influential in establishing Christianity, along with its standards and guidelines, as a central component of her personality. Academics appealed less to her. "I didn't like school," she said. "At that time, learning was memorizing. Like a robot, we were not taught to have our own minds. Students sat in neat rows with our heads down. During tests, we regurgitated topics from memory, repeating words without knowing anything about them. We sounded like turkeys."

Silvya's best instruction happened outside of the classroom. "I remember playing with my friends from school and with my cousins, many of whom lived in the city. We were always outside, taking advantage of Cochabamba's always spring-like conditions."

Much later in her life, she purchased an apartment in Cochabamba. Whenever she returned to her country to visit family or simply to reconnect, she would stay there. The environment—the warmth, the people, the ice cream parlors, and the fresh freesia flowers blooming along the Paseo El Prado, the town's main boulevard—connected her with fond memories from her past.

HUMBERTÓ'S POST IN Cochabamba lasted just over a year. In 1944, he accepted his next position as commander of the Bolivian Military Academy in La Paz, the institute he had graduated from two decades earlier. He purchased a house in the city's Sopocachi neighborhood. "Our home was very happy, simple, and well-protected," Silvya said. "It had a nice front yard filled with beautiful roses, fruit trees, and pine trees which created a wall to protect us." She added, "Curiously, Hans Kundt was a previous owner." This detail provided an intriguing contrast as Humbertó viewed himself as the military and philosophical opposite of the former German general.

The home's location was its primary advantage. It was situated on a hill, surrounded by empty space, and just three blocks from the Plaza Abaroa which is among the most central places in La Paz. From their garden, the family enjoyed expansive city views, a complete panorama including downtown La Paz with the top of Mt. Illimani off in the distance.

In many ways, commanding the Military Academy represented the peak of Humbertó's professional aspiration. He viewed the cadets as family. Above all, he was loyal to them, and he vowed to protect them while they were enrolled at his institution.

During his tenure as commander, a political unrest tested Humbertó's conviction. Protestors had congregated in the Plaza Murillo. They threatened to storm the government buildings surrounding the plaza including the national congress and the presidential palace. Humbertó received orders to march his cadets to central La Paz to join enlisted soldiers who had been deployed to defend the government. Believing the cadets were more student than soldier, he ignored the order and demanded the doors to the academy be bolted shut.

These actions, while unpopular with some of his superior officers, enhanced his standing with the cadets as well as some politicians. Professors from the local *Universidad de San Andres* were equally impressed. In Humbertó, they saw the promise of someone who could bridge the gap separating Bolivia's working classes from the political and military elite.

In December 1943, General Gualberto Villarroel López stepped into the Bolivian presidency. He ascended to this position after orchestrating a coup to overthrow his predecessor, Enrique Peñaranda—another former general who had served as head of the Bolivian military during the later stages of the Chaco War.

History recalls Villarroel as a president who favored reform. During his term in office, Bolivia took substantive steps to legitimize Bolivian workers' unions, establish pensions, and abolish the practice of *mit'a*, a form of unpaid servitude with roots extending back to the time of the Inca. To expand his populist appeal, Villarroel created a coalition with the Movimiento Nacionalista Revolucionario. This move was particularly significant as this new political party's appeal was expanding rapidly among both workers and intellectuals.

It is also noteworthy the United States suspected Villarroel of pro-Axis sympathies. Because of this, the US initially did not recognize his presidency, and changed this stance only after Villarroel agreed to sever ties with the MNR. Villarroel stepped it up by taking repressive measures against the MNR including arresting and deporting many of the party's leaders. While this maneuvering may have increased his standing with the US government, it damaged his domestic popularity. Villarroel's failure to maintain support among the increasingly vocal and mobilized working class proved to be a fatal flaw. This same characteristic may also have been the greatest weakness of the politicians and military men who were allied with him.

FROM THE VANTAGE point of her protected world, Silvya formed her own impression of Gualberto Villarroel López. She judged him and other members of Bolivia's ruling class—a small clique of military men and dignitaries—not based on any political agenda, but instead using the simple standards of youth. Certainly, she was influenced by her parents' words and ideals. Also, and without trying, she trusted the feelings and thoughts she experienced in the presence of these people. She paid attention to how nice they were to her, and how well they treated her family.

"Villarroel and my father attended the military academy together," she said. "They were good friends." Attempting to express the depth of this friendship, she added, "You have to understand, only a certain type of person made it to the academy." In Bolivia, as it is often the case in many places around the world, who you are—your background and pedigree—helps to determine who you will become.

Beyond their shared foundation, Humbertó's and Gualberto's friendship transcended any social status they may have shared. As is the case with almost any class of people who have huddled together in close quarters for an extended period, or experienced life-defining moments of hardship or personal growth together, they formed a bond. Their friendship extended beyond the time they spent together as cadets and continued throughout the duration of their careers.

"Villarroel's wife was also a very good friend of my mother's," Silvya said, "and I went to school with their children. On many occasions, we received invitations to birthdays and elegant tea parties with their family." These parties took place in beautiful and safe environments—everything carefully planned to ensure the children received the best care, privilege, and love. The parents' unspoken objective was to encourage their children to interact with each other. They were also insulating the children from the tumultuous events unfolding just beyond this pristine world.

CHAPTER 10

Santiago

Chilean border from the Bolivian Altiplano, 2011

*"All paths lead to the same goal: to convey to others
what we are. And we must pass through solitude
and difficulty, isolation and silence in order to reach
forth to the enchanted place where we can dance
our clumsy dance and sing our sorrowful song."*

—PABLO NERUDA

TWO YEARS INTO his post as commander of the military academy in La Paz, Bolivia's military leaders once again asked Humbertó to move. In part as a reflection of his friendship with President Villarroel, he received an enviable appointment as Bolivia's military attaché to its neighbor and former adversary, Chile.

From 1946 to 1948, Humbertó and his family lived in Santiago. Silvya recalled, "We had an elegant house, complete with a smoking room, many beautiful paintings, and a large library filled with books." Her parents had rented the home from a prominent Chilean politician, military officer and historian, Aquiles Vergara Vicuña. Siding with Bolivia, Vicuña had served in the Chaco War. He had also authored a controversial account of the South American War of the Pacific. In this book, he concluded Chile should not have taken the sea from Bolivia.

Unsurprisingly, Humbertó was attracted to this perspective. "Vicuña became a very good friend of my father," Silvya said. "He was interesting, intelligent, and with principles that would not bend."

TODAY, SILVYA RETAINS a collection of photos that capture details from her family's time in Chile. They depict formal settings—galas and dinners with dignitaries and other seemingly important people. "Mainly, it was a social experience," she said. "My parents had to represent Bolivia to the Chileans. I remember the parties. They took over our entire house. My brother, sister, and I went to the basement. We ate our dinner there, sitting on crate boxes. After eating, we'd make playhouses with the crates. The parties would often last long into the night, so we'd sleep down there."

"It wasn't bad," she added. "We had a good life, just not enough privacy. My father wished he could go back to Bolivia. Our comfortable home, and his status—he was willing to put all of this aside."

Demands on Humbertó made the time he spent with his family even more precious. As often as possible, he would read to his children—tales of great adventures by Defoe and Dumas—*Robinson Crusoe, The Count of Monte Cristo, The Three Musketeers.* "I would fall asleep thinking about these stories and comforted by my father's voice. Later, these memories and my own desire to experience new things made it easier for me to leave Bolivia."

SOLDIER, COMMANDER OF the military academy, military attaché— Humbertó welcomed all his posts as honors as well as his duty. As an officer, it was not his place to question the reasons behind these mandates. When tasked to do something, he was loyalty-bound to follow orders. He perceived each of his assignments as opportunities to serve his country. Humbly, he also saw them as fortunate chances to assert his allegiance to his superior officers, many of whom had helped guide him from his time as a cadet, through the Chaco War, to Italy, and beyond.

Silvya now suspects these requests to move her father from post to post were just a ruse masking attempts to silence him by distancing him from the La Paz political scene. "My father had to go to Chile, because he was ordered to. Some people perceived him as trouble, and perhaps more loyal to his soldiers and the values he shared with them than he was to any bureaucracy.

"Around this time, it was becoming clear other groups—political parties, professors from the university, and others within the military—wanted him to take the presidency. To keep him from gaining more control, they sent him to Santiago." Humbertó had become a playing piece in the unpredictable game to determine who would lead Bolivia.

TWO-AND-ONE-HALF YEARS INTO his presidency—a longer tenure than most of his predecessors—a changing political tide forced President Villarroel out of office. Unpopular with his constituents for having turned against the MNR in favor of the US and realizing his political prospects were doomed, Villarroel had few options.

Before Villarroel faded into the recesses of Latin American history, even before he was able to leave the *Palacio Quemado*—the official residence of the president of Bolivia, located in the Plaza

Murillo and nicknamed the Burned Palace because it had once been set ablaze—a citizen mob forced its way into the building. The horde assassinated the president along with several of his aides. Villarroel's body was thrown out of a window and down to the cobblestone pavement three stories below. The mob stripped the clothing off his body and hoisted it to the top of a telephone pole.

There he was, the president of the republic. There he was, human and fragile. There he was, Gualberto Villarroel López, soldier and would be populist, rejected by the citizens of La Paz, disrobed and on display for everyone to see. And there it was, the justice of an oppressed people.

HUMBERTÓ AND HIS family were visiting La Paz during the upheaval. On the day of Villarroel's assassination, they were scheduled to return to Chile. While heading for the airport in El Alto, they heard about the uprising over a local station, Radio Aspiazu. They were accustomed to hearing bad news. Still, the violence and barbarism seemed unbelievable. Certain this was false information, Humbertó detoured with his family to pass by the Plaza Murillo.

The incredible proved true. Silvya reflected, "I remember seeing the president hanging by a pole in front of the cathedral." She also recalled her mother's hands flashing over her eyes to shield her from the gruesome spectacle. Thinking back seventy years later, she struggled to determine if it was her mother's horror, or the hanging bodies that branded that moment in her memory.

CHAPTER 11

Roboré

Bolivian jungle, 2011

> "Green, how I want you green.
> Green wind. Green branches."

—FEDERICO GARCÍA LORCA, *ROMANCE SONÁMBULO*

WHILE MOST BOLIVIANS live in the Altiplano, or in cities situated in the valleys leading up to it, the majority of the country's landmass exists in the lowlands. Encompassing roughly the same surface area as the state of Texas, this is a vast yet sparsely populated expanse. Water from Andean glaciers flows down to the cloud forests. This water fuses with runoff from these forests to form rivers. The Guaporé, the Mamoré, the Beni, the Pilcomayo, and the *Madre de Diós*—the Mother of God—are among Bolivia's principal waterways. These rivers meander down to grasslands and jungles until connecting with the mightiest of the South American rivers, the Amazon or the Plata, and finally to the Atlantic Ocean. Along these routes, minerals that were scraped off mountain peaks are redeposited back into the soil to create the foundation for one of the world's most biodiverse regions.

Bolivia is home to 17,000 species of seed plants—from *ichu*, a coarse thatching grass, to *pará*, the rubber tree. You'll find a rainbow-array of more than 4,000 varieties of potatoes—this root vege-table, incidentally, was first domesticated by people who lived in present-day Bolivia and Peru more than 7,000 years ago. There are also more than 2,900 animal species, including 398 mammals, 1,400 birds, 277 reptiles, 204 amphibians, and 635 fish. (Wikipedia 2019) Much of this diversity resides in tropical forests—the cloud forests of the La Paz and Cochabamba departments, and the jungles of the Beni, Pando, Tarija, and Santa Cruz departments. This biological abundance benefits from the country's sparse population and remote location.

Thick vegetation, rugged terrain, and uncharted places provide cover for nefarious activities. Virtually all the coca leaves cultivated, and all the cocaine produced in the world, originates from three countries, Colombia, Peru, and Bolivia. The majority of Bolivia's coca crop is grown in two regions: the Yungas and Chapare cloud forests. The refinement of cocaine—a tedious process transforming leaves to paste, and then to powder—happens in well-hidden places.

While Bolivia deserves its reputation as a safe destination for tourists, meandering in the coca growing regions is ill-advised. People disappear. They may slip and fall while trekking, or they might stumble across activities they were not intended to discover. One well-chronicled incident occurred in 1986. While conducting field work in the Huanchaca National Park in Bolivia near the Brazilian border, a group of scientists led by a renowned local biologist and environmentalist, Noel Kempff Mercado, happened upon a cocaine factory. Mercado, along with most of the members of his group, was killed. Curiously, this act of violence helped preserve the park in perpetuity.

In 1988, Huanchaca Park was renamed Noel Kempff Mercado National Park. Famed for its pristine vegetation and expansive selection of endangered animal species, all of which have remained largely spared from human intervention, UNESCO designated this park a World Heritage Site in 2000. The UNESCO website boasts Noel Kempff is one of the largest and most intact parks in the Amazon basin. The organization also touts the park's rich evolutionary history, which extends over a billion years.

FROM THE ALTIPLANO, there are three primary ways to access the Bolivian lowlands. For a fee that westerners would deem nominal, but many locals would consider a small fortune, you can catch an Amazonas Airline flight from El Alto to Bolivian jungle towns including Rurrenebaque, Trinidad and Riberalta. These towns epitomize stereotypical South American sleepiness—the *mañana culture,* which is the notion there is no need to do anything today that can, and probably should, be postponed until tomorrow.

The towns are positioned as launching pads for deeper ventures into the Amazonian backcountry. Location, seclusion, and obscurity are among the reasons why they have become tourist destinations. They are fixtures on a *gringo trail* frequented by Americans, Europeans, Israelis, and others who are temporarily escaping from their first world challenges or decompressing after completing obligatory military service.

It takes less than an hour by air to travel from La Paz to the Bolivian jungle. The airplane deployed is small and propeller driven. It resembles the aircraft used by the Uruguayan rugby team on their ill-fated crossing of the Andes in October 1972, a trip well-chronicled in the book and film *Alive.* Due to poor piloting, most of those players and their friends did not complete the journey. Their plane crashed, and the survivors turned to their faith, and eventually cannibalism, to endure the harsh Andean conditions for ten weeks. (Read 2005)

Making a similar air journey across the Andes—as turbulence sets in, and while peering through tiny windows paned with aged glass sporting a yellow tinge that is just clear enough to see through—thoughts of those Uruguayans might cross your mind.

The opportunity to witness up close, the peaks of the Andean goliaths surrounding La Paz—Illimani, Huayna Potosí, Ancohuma, and Mururata—justifies the flight. From the air, you can almost touch the glaciers perched on top of these mountains. The view is simultaneously spectacular and unsettling—*is it possible to safely fly so close to peaks as magnificent and formidable as these?*

FOR THE BUDGET traveler, the ubiquitous Bolivian *autobus* is the preferred way to make this journey. While other bus routes within the country offer semi-luxurious options—including fully reclining *bus cama*, or bus bed seats, and an uninterrupted stream of action films—the *autobus* route from La Paz into the jungle exemplifies ordinary, no-frills transportation. The standard experience takes place on an older bus that once was a school bus in some North American city. While traveling on one of these busses—which were designed to accommodate thirty children—and while seated on a bench chair made of kid-proof vinyl, you are joined by forty-five other people, and often some of their livestock. The duration of this journey makes the experience noteworthy. The road trip from La Paz to Rurrenebaque is advertised as taking twelve hours, but most often it takes twenty-four.

Despite the uncomfortable seating on a jungle-bound bus, the trip is unforgettable. The initial portion—the first sixty miles separating La Paz from the next sizable town—takes about three hours. As the route begins on the outskirts of La Paz, a priest enters the bus. He's there to bless the people onboard, and to prepare their souls for the prospect this day could be their last. The blessing is appropriate as Bolivia is a Roman Catholic country. It also makes sense because the road is one of the most hazardous in the world. The Inter American Bank designated it THE world's most dangerous road. (Nag 2017) Like warning labels on cigarette boxes, the name tourists have attached to it delivers more direct guidance. It is the Death Road. Each year, this short section of compressed South American dirt claims around three hundred lives.

The priest departs the bus, and like a car on an antique roller coaster, the vehicle quickly ratchets up to the top of a mountain pass. Called *La Cumbre*, or The Summit, the pass sits at an ever-frozen 15,000 feet above sea level. While still dwarfed by the adjacent mountains, this pass approximates the height of Mt. Blanc, the highest point in western Europe. Beyond *La Cumbre*, the road drops… down, down, down until reaching Coroico, the next outpost on the path to the jungle.

The width of the Death Road is almost enough to accommodate one-way traffic. The road's designers, nevertheless, did not intend for it to be used for single-direction travel. Busses and flatbed trucks, large vehicles filled with fresh fruit and humans shipping to and from the lowlands, speed back and forth along the road. Sometimes, they pass a bit too close to each other. When this happens, the vehicle closest to the edge loses.

The road's precarious placement enhances its infamous reputation. Clinging to the sides of cliffs, and passing directly underneath waterfalls, it meanders along the muddy edge of the Bolivian Andes. On wet days—which unsurprisingly occur regularly in the cloud forest—these waterfalls may surge and wash away large chunks of road. Anything resting on top—a hapless animal or a vehicle brimming with passengers—goes tumbling into the abyss.

THERE IS A safer, yet slower and more unforgettable way to make this journey from La Paz to the jungle. People have been employing it since pre-Colombian times. Back then, artisan-laborers crafted great roads with stones so thoughtfully placed that even today, after centuries of heavy weather and dramatic tectonic movements, they retain their impressive structure and form. Very few examples of modern-day construction compare to the quality and durability of this ancient Andean infrastructure.

The trek by foot from La Paz to Coroico takes about three days. Most people spend the first night camping close to the starting point at *La Cumbre*. There are no hard-set rules stipulating where sleeping is permissible. An individual's best personal judgment serves as the guide. You are free to enter the many structures sitting along the road. You can run your hands across the stone-slab walls which were cut by hand, and moved into

Top of the Cumbre to Coroico trail, 1996. Author's tents visible in the ruins in the foreground

position with ingenuity, yet without the assistance of the wheel, a tool that didn't make it to the Americas until after European colonialization. On the sides of these walls, you can see, even smell, the stains from ancient wood fires. In this space created for and by travelers from a distant time, you can gaze at the unobstructed stars of the Milky Way, peering back billions of years to when time began. There cannot be a better place to experience this.

On the second day, the trail passes through villages that have never known vehicles, electricity, or running water. Local children approach passing hikers like gawkers observing exotic animals in a zoo. This is their turf, and hikers are the outsiders.

The jungle arrives on the third day. Hints of its presence materialize in advance. You begin to feel the thickening air miles before you sense a rise in temperature. Wisps of moisture invade cloudless skies. Eventually, dense foliage accomplishes what a half-millennium of earthquakes could not. The jungle engulfs the ancient road. The trek shifts course to follow a trail with a width just suitable to accommodate a single individual. As you are hiking, a passing llama or villager periodically disrupts your rhythm forcing you to quickly and carefully step aside to allow them to pass.

Step-by-step, this is the best way to experience the transition from the big skies, desert, and snow of the Altiplano to the flowing water and lush vegetation of a cloud forest. It is easier to grasp the substance of this change when progressing slowly with all senses engaged.

HUMBERTÓ'S NEXT ASSIGNMENT moved him from Santiago, Chile down to the jungles of Bolivia. Back then, the Bolivian Army was, as it remains today, organized into ten territorial divisions. Each of these roughly aligned with the country's nine constituent departments—Beni, Cochabamba, La Paz, Oruro, Potosí, Santa Cruz, Sucre, Tarija, and Trinidad. With this latest post, the army tasked Humbertó to lead its Fifth Division which encompassed much of Santa Cruz, the country's largest department.

Everything appeared to be on track. Step-by-step, following an erratic course that bounced across the country and spanned continents, Humbertó continued to climb up the military hierarchy. The politicians responsible for delivering his assignments may have had different goals. Distancing Humbertó from the action in La Paz may have reflected their desire to control the decisions and doings that determined how the country was governed, and who would lead it.

IN 1949, HUMBERTÓ, Alicia and their three children made the trek to Roboré, a remote outpost half-way between Santa Cruz de la Sierra, the department's capital city, and the Brazilian border. Silvya recalled this as a jovial time. Always surrounded by nature, it was one of the best of her life. "Roboré was a cute little town," she said. "Everything was built around a plaza which had a church in its center. We lived in a house just off the plaza. Nearby, there was the army barracks, the municipal building, a few shops, and a *cancha* or playing field. My school was next to the church."

Flaunting the tropical setting, the plaza was lined with palm trees. In the center, there was a pergola where children would romp around. On Sundays, the local military band would play there.

Silvya's days began with the sound of crowing roosters. Local troops of howler monkeys announced their presence with groans and grunts that thump you like a wave. Nighttime was alive with the cacophony of chirping insects. Thunderous yet soothing this chorus assisted her passage to a perfect sleep.

Life was simple. "I used to walk to school," she continued. "On weekends, my mother, siblings, and I would go to the market to get ice cream. Everything was within a few steps of our house."

Alicia allowed her daughter to adopt a capuchin monkey who Silvya named, *Petiti*. Alicia was a steadfast devotee to all—or as it turned out, most—furry creatures. While Petiti's daily exploits and adventures entertained the children, Alicia was unimpressed. Petiti was unkempt. He also carried an unshakable odor that seemed to have been sourced from the bowels of the jungle.

In addition to forest creatures, Silvya was also surrounded by human companions. She was nice enough, and well-capable of creating lasting relationships with her peers. And yet, she acknowledges, as the commander's daughter, it was easier for her to attract attention and company than it was for her fellow schoolmates.

Not far from town, a river flowed. Locals claimed its thermal waters held medicinal qualities. Mostly, it was a place of leisure. Silvya said, "our chauffeur would drive me and my friends there after school. I remember the beautiful stones in the riverbed. They felt soft on your feet, as if they were welcoming you. No one else was there. It was our own special place to play, and to be separated from adults."

WHILE HIS FAMILY explored their new environment, Humbertó was busy establishing structure and procedure in this largely unpopulated and ungoverned corner of eastern Bolivia. His primary responsibility was to secure the vast border with Brazil. As the prospect of a conflict between the two countries was quite limited, his work centered on establishing a permanent military presence there.

Building a military base—the same barracks Silvya recalled from her childhood memories—was his first task. He also introduced municipal improvements. Monumentally, he was the first person to bring electricity to the town, and he was the first to drop a water well. As many places around the world are named after people who have impacted them, so too does this town reflect his legacy. While Roboré still, rather pleasantly, barely registers on maps, its central corridor—the area surrounding the plaza—retains the official name, Humbertó Torres Ortíz.

After completing the municipal improvements, Humbertó's work shifted to monitoring the territory for any intrusion. This largely uneventful task involved multi-day expeditions into the *campo*, the boundless space beyond electricity and sterility. Silvya joined her father on one of these trips. Their caravan of trucks, soldiers, and supplies traveled along a newly inaugurated road. At night, they sought respite in camps pitched next to the famed Jesuit Missions of the Chiquitos, which collectively have since been designated by UNESCO as a World Heritage Site. These missions have Christian names that juxtapose their native environment— San Francisco Javier, Concepción, Santa Ana, San Miguel, San Rafael and San José. Their architecture blends indigenous stylings with European religious heritage and reflects the history and complexity of the Bolivian Chiquitanía territory.

Toward the end of the journey, the convoy of soldiers stopped alongside the road. They had arrived at a place that retained its raw jungle nature and was separated from the virtues of religious oversight. Their mission had changed.

Silvya said, "For some reason which I can't recall, a soldier from the barracks got lost in the jungle. My father and his men set out to search for him."

They found the soldier. The smell of his decaying body betrayed his resting spot. It appeared he had become the target of a hunt most likely led by a group of indigenous locals. He had strayed away from the safety of his battalion.

A misstep.

This could have happened to anyone.

The soldier's demise resulted from the aggression of an unknown band of insurgents. It was an act seemingly without cause and without consequence. It also exposed the shadow of a mounting unrest building within the country.

CHAPTER 12

Comandante General

Plaza Murillo in La Paz, 2011

*"Out beyond ideas of wrongdoing and right
doing there is a field. I'll meet you there."*

—RUMI

IN THE LATE 1940s, approximately three million people lived in Bolivia. Eighty percent resided in the western third of the country in and around the cities of La Paz, Cochabamba, Oruro, Sucre and Potosí. Most of these people were illiterate. Many were miners or other disgruntled members of the indigenous class. Increasingly, these marginalized Bolivians rejected their circumstances. They scorned the concept of a small group of moneyed people with European heritage controlling them. They rallied behind a shared conviction these elites, and their ancestors before them, had stolen indigenous land and exploited native resources.

People mobilized under the banner of the reformist Movimiento Nacionalista Revolucionario party. They joined forces with dissidents from the urban middle-class along with professors, journalists, and artisans to demand reforms including improved working conditions, and a redistribution of the country's land and resources back to indigenous owners.

From 1943 to 1946, Paz Estenssoro, representing the MNR, served as finance minister in Gualberto Villarroel's cabinet. He escaped Villarroel's brutal fate by moving to Argentina where, under the protection of Juan Perón, he lived in exile. In 1947, Paz Estenssoro ran for president of Bolivia against Enrique Hertzog, a medical doctor representing the Republican Socialist Union Party. Despite the left-leaning sound of their party's name, Hertzog and the Republican Socialists pursued a vision of returning Bolivia to the nationalist state that existed before the Chaco War. Their presidential campaign, and their party's charter, focused on safeguarding Bolivia from the true socialists, a consortium of subversive groups which included the MNR.

Hertzog won this round, and from 1947 to 1949 he served as president. Many of his subjects would debate the use of the word, "served." MNR party activists along with unionized miners and laborers were targeted by police raids, punished into submission, or deported from the country.

Despite these efforts, Hertzog failed to achieve his vision. Recognizing the growing divide separating elected leaders from their constituents as well as his weakened status within his own party, in 1949, he stepped down from the presidency. Preferring a moderate as his successor, he turned to Humbertó.

Less well-known, but unwavering in his loyalty to Bolivia, Humbertó shared some of Hertzog's aspirations for the country. Humbertó's unwavering belief in the separation of state and military affairs, however, prohibited him from pursuing the presidency. As an alternative, Hertzog selected Bolivia's aggressive and combative vice president, Mamerto Urriolagoitía.

◆ ◆ ◆

ROUND TWO, THE presidential election of 1950, pitted Urriolagoitía against Paz Estenssoro and the surging popularity of the MNR.
This time, Paz Estenssoro won. He succeeded despite a substantial
handicap caused by a Bolivian law extending voting rights exclusively to a small minority of *latifundistas*, the Latin American equivalent of the landed gentry.

But in politics, winning is sometimes a point of opinion.

Urriolagoitía rejected the election results, claiming his rival had
never received the fifty-one percent of votes required for a decision.
Without this majority, according to law, the reins of the government
were to pass to the Bolivian Congress. It is unlikely Urriolagoitía
ever intended this transfer of power to occur.

On June 16, 1951, in an act that would become known as the,
"Mamertazo" of Bolivian politics, Urriolagoitía ceded control to a
temporary government, a *junta* consisting of three generals: Hugo
Ballivián Rojas, who had served as commander of the Bolivian
Armed Forces under Urriolagoitía, Antonió Seleme Vargas, a career
officer and former head of the nation's military police, and Humbertó Torres Ortíz. These men promised to deliver an election to
the people of Bolivia, and they affirmed their intent to hand the
government back to the people. They also promised to halt what
they feared was an attempted Sovietization of Bolivia.

The MNR retrenched, and Paz Estenssoro was forced into exile
in Peru.

Ballivián and Seleme asked Humbertó to lead the *junta*. They
shared many of his ideals and were attracted to his impeccable background. They also sensed Humbertó could be used to attract more
support for their cause.

For the second time, Humbertó declined the opportunity to
lead his country. "Precisely because he was in the military," Silvya

said. "This was his career, not politics." Convinced that by joining the *junta* he could help influence a positive outcome, he agreed to return from Roboré to La Paz to accept an appointment as *commandante general*, commander in chief, and major general of the armed forces. Humbertó and Ballivián selected Seleme as secretary of state. Completing the team, Humbertó and Seleme looked to Ballivián to lead the *junta*. The three generals remained in power for the next eleven months.

SILVYA'S MEMORIES OF the men and the politics from this era are pieced together from personal experiences, family photos, and the stories shared by her family. "When I see pictures from this time, I remember," she said. "I can even hear my father talking to these people or talking about them. Of course, back then, I was young. I didn't care about politics. Now, some of those experiences become clear. They mean more to me."

A few memories stand out. Humbertó once shared a story with her. Many years before, when he and Paz Estenssoro were both still young, not long after Humbertó graduated from the military academy, the two men were traveling together on a train. Paz Estenssoro was recruiting promising people from the army to get involved in politics. He knocked on Humbertó's cabin door. "On that train ride, Paz Estenssoro tried to enlist my father," Silvya said. "My father did not believe in, and could never support, military officials becoming involved in politics. Paz Estenssoro's proposal left my father with a bad impression of him."

Flash forward to 1951. Despite his hesitations and principles, Humbertó was now braided into the political establishment.

Silvya remarked, "My father did not like how Urriolagoitía would not cede power to the elected government. Still he viewed the MNR as leftist and dangerous. Because of this, he believed the *junta* was justified."

Silvya shared additional memories of the men who formed the *junta*. "While my father felt he could influence Ballivián, and help direct the government toward the appropriate outcome, my mother was less confident. She believed my father's role was dangerous."

Alicia perceived a lack of trust among the members of the *junta*. Despite their outbound expression of togetherness, she could sense they were not united in their mission. "Seleme used to come to my house," Silvya said. "My mother didn't like him. She would say, 'he does not look you in the eyes.' She shared this opinion with my father, but he was blinded by his faith in people. He always saw the best in them."

Ultimately, Alicia's intuition was accurate. The new government's principles, and any purity of vision its leaders may have possessed took a back seat to their egos. Friends became enemies. The goal of preserving an individual's status within the society supplanted adherence to any bonds of loyalty, integrity or dignity that may have existed before they came together to lead the nation.

In February 1952, Humbertó asked the MNR for a truce. He promised early elections and confirmed his willingness to pursue constitutional reforms that would favor the working class. Behind the scenes, and contrary to his counter-revolutionary pedigree, Seleme had already been negotiating with the MNR. Humbertó and General Ballivián discovered this and dismissed Seleme from their ranks. The damage was already done.

On April 9, 1952, the Wednesday before Easter Sunday and the day Seleme was released of his command, the *junta* lost control of the military police force stationed in La Paz. Maintaining control had been a critical element in a broader strategy to establish discipline and solidify authority. Recognizing the significance of this loss, Humbertó rushed from his home in La Paz to an army base in El Alto to assemble an army unit to fill the void left by the vacated police.

While Humbertó was in El Alto, Seleme tasked the La Paz police, who still looked to him for direction, to seize control of the city. Siding with the police, armed militias fashioned from workers' unions joined the struggle.

To resist the uprising, Humbertó assembled eight-thousand troops. Many of these soldiers defected. Some of the men were disgruntled; others calculated the opposing side stood a better chance of winning.

FOR SILVYA, THE revolution started unremarkably. "I remember waking up in the morning to the sound of my mother speaking on the phone with my father," she said. "He had left our home very early. I didn't know where he was, or why he was gone, but I could tell she was worried."

Her mother's concerns were justified. Her husband had left to fight a civil war. More than a year would pass before she would see him again.

Shortly after the call, sounds of the conflict began to echo through the streets of La Paz. "The location of our home was interesting," Silvya said. "We lived on a hill with a 360-degree view of La Paz. We could easily see the Avenida 6 de Agosto and the Parque Laikacota. In the beginning, the fighting seemed to concentrate around this area. We could see the soldiers and hear the fire from their guns. Some bullets even hit our house."

The battle spread. Alicia's oldest brother, Criso, arrived to retrieve her and her children. Wanting to ward off any looters, Alicia decided to stay at home. Gloria, Silvya, and Gustavo walked with their uncle for ten blocks to their aunt Betty's home. Under any other circumstance, this would have been a leisurely outing.

"Very few people were in the streets, but the shooting continued," Silvya said. "We were told to keep our heads down and move quickly. My family was well-known in La Paz, and certainly in our neighborhood. Mobs had begun looting. They were targeting the homes and businesses of families who were thought to be loyal to the government."

Criso and the children walked through a park. "I could see blood, and what I think were human fingers dangling from the trees," Silvya said. Surviving the gauntlet, they arrived at Betty's house terrified but safe.

Other family members shared their stories of the Revolution. Silvya's cousin Zonia, who was seven at the time, recalled bullets whistling over her head as she ran with her parents through the streets of La Paz. "There were bodies hanging in the plazas," she said.

As the number of available soldiers in the Altiplano was limited, the army called on cadets from the military academy to rush from Ingavi, south of the city, to defend La Paz. It is unclear who ordered the cadets to engage. As this was contrary to his character, it is hard to imagine Humbertó initiated the order. As commander in chief, he was ultimately responsible. Regardless of the origin of the command, perhaps as an expression of last resort, cadets marched into the city along the Avenida Busch in the city's Miraflores neighborhood. They passed in front of the home of Silvya's cousin Gabriel. "A cadet was shot in front of my house," he said. "My parents pulled him inside. He survived!"

One small victory.

Gabriel's family lived across the street from the headquarters of the Falange Socialista Boliviana, a right-wing political party and principal adversary of the MNR. The Falangistas, as the members of this group were known, endured a brutal bombardment. Bullets from as close as across the street fused with heavy artillery shot from across the city.

The building was torn apart.

On April 11, 1952, three days after the fighting began, the revolution ended. A coalition of MNR party members, unionists, and intellectuals defeated the *junta* along with the entirety of the Bolivian armed forces. Fleeing his holdout near El Alto, military loyalists ushered Humbertó across the border into Peru.

General Seleme also left the country. Soon after, he returned to Bolivia. Having crafted an agreement with Hernán Siles Zuazo from the MNR, Seleme expected he would ascend to the presidency. Instead, the revolutionaries summoned Paz Estenssoro back from exile in Argentina, and placed him into his rightful, elected position as the president of the Republic of Bolivia. Hernán Siles Zuazo became vice president.

It wasn't supposed to turn out this way, or at least, this wasn't the outcome Humbertó had hoped for.

As PROMISED, PAZ Estenssoro and his new government quickly initiated a wave of reforms. They established universal suffrage and removed the voting requirements of literacy and property ownership. They instituted a program of redistribution of rural property—land that in many cases had been owned by families for generations went back to indigenous ownership. They also nationalized the country's three largest mining operators—Grupo Hochschild, Grupo Aramayo, and by far the largest of the three, Simón Patiño's Grupo Patiño. The government consolidated these holdings under the newly created *Corporación Minera de Bolivia,* The Mining Corporation of Bolivia, or COMIBOL. A government of the people and for the people, the MNR, it appeared, was poised to address Bolivians' long-standing grievances. Yet, one decade later, the movement lost momentum.

The costs of running the expanding bureaucracy, which included orchestrating the bulk of the country's economic activity, placed an untenable burden on the government. This led to economic instability. From 1952 to 1956, Paz Estenssoro's first term, inflation increased by almost two hundred percent. (Sachs 1989, 59). During the same period, the number of workers employed by COMIBOL increased from 24,000 to about 36,000. Inversely, the corporation's production declined by about 20 percent. (Mahmod Ali Ayub 1985, 14)

The Bolivian political pendulum continued to swing. From 1956 to 1960, Siles Zuazo, stepped into the presidency. Paz Estenssoro served again from 1960 to 1964. At the end of his second term, he attempted to secure an additional, consecutive term.

This round, the conservatives, led by General René Barrientos Ortuño, intervened. Playing a classic Bolivian hand, they orchestrated a coup resulting in the overthrow of the MNR. The country returned to military rule. It remained this way for much of the next twenty years.

CHAPTER 13

Exile

In flight in front of the Palacio Quemando, La Paz, 2011

"I am a man, and the sky is immense."

—OCTAVIO PAZ

H UMBERTÓ'S MOVE TO Arequipa was a cold start. Within a week, he went from running a country to running from it. He left everything behind—his family, status, income, and pension. As a civil servant, his means had always reflected his profession. Evading all illusions of a *caudillo* living lavishly in exile, he commenced a meager lifestyle.

He took jobs with the local municipality; regular jobs, earning just enough to pay his rent and purchase his food. He worked as a surveyor, tasked with measuring and recording the land in and around Arequipa. Later, he worked for the Arequipa Lottery, writing and sometimes delivering advertisements through local radio.

A few weeks after arriving in Peru, he learned Seleme, his former comrade, had publicly accused him of conspiring against Ballivián and the military *junta*. Compelled to dispel these accusations, he began writing his own account of the events leading up to the revolution. He composed a manifesto—a several-thousand-word-attempt to clear his name. He had nothing to lose, and not much to gain. He knew he would never again lead his country. All he could do was try to represent himself and his legacy honorably.

Humbertó addressed the opening paragraph, "To the people of Bolivia and the nation's armed forces." He went on to detail the circumstances and sentiments that led him to accept his appointment to the *junta*. Before then, he had led a satisfying career. Having served as commander of the military academy in La Paz, and then as the general in charge of the army's Fifth Division in Roboré, he had already realized the peak of his professional ambitions. He was preparing to retire. "I had achieved all that was required for me to do this," he wrote.

By submitting his request to retire, he attracted the attention of government officials. Several of these people visited him in the Bolivian subtropics, including a former Bolivian commander in chief, General Armando Sainz Iturri. Outright, General Sainz Iturri rejected Humbertó's request, citing "the loyalty a soldier owes to his army." Sainz Iturri asserted, Humbertó had more to do. The nation needed his labor as well as his loyalty. Sainz Iturri ordered—not requested—Humbertó to step up to an expanded leadership position, and to help Bolivia navigate the troubling circumstances resulting from the 1950 election.

Humbertó wrote, "I accepted this role because there was still hope I could find a solution" —to the political situation facing the nation— "and preserve the prestige of the army." He believed Urriolagoitia's maneuvering during the election—the Mamertazo of Bolivian politics—damaged the army's status and dignity along with the honor of all the men who served in it. He was also aware that if he were to disobey the order, he would be held accountable for the outcome, whatever it might be.

Humbertó left Roboré for La Paz to meet with General Ballivián. During the meeting, he did not recoil from voicing his concerns. "I am the number one enemy of the military *junta*," Humbertó declared. "My main objective is to maneuver the government back to a general election.... I accept this position, but I do so reluctantly. I believe I am better informed than you are about our situation. Events can happen in the very short-term that will carry unpleasant consequences for our country. I know my presence in the headquarters of the general staff can improve the situation.

"On the other hand," Humbertó continued, "I know I am going into this as a sacrifice, putting my sword, once again, at the service of the army and Bolivia. I go to serve, but not to serve myself."

FOR HUMBERTÓ, IT became evident early on that some of the people who swarmed around the *junta* were more intent on ensuring positive outcomes for themselves, than pursuing any beneficial policies or ideals they purportedly backed. These men maneuvered the political uncertainty and hedged their bets by taking secretive meetings and forming clandestine alliances with the MNR. Preferring pragmatism over division, he had pushed aside any concerns about his colleagues. "I began to adhere to my customary work rhythm," he wrote, "while recognizing the enormous responsibility I had assumed during an exceptionally serious and delicate moment." He had also observed the concerns of his fellow citizens. "Because Urriolagoitia had put the government in our hands, a faction within the population believed authority continued to reside with him."

Urriolagoitia had fallen out of favor with these citizens. They feared the *junta*-led government would call upon the former president, or that he would call upon himself, to once again lead the nation. Moreover, the people maintained the *junta* was unconstitutional. Humbertó wrote, "Making common cause with my immediate collaborators" —Ballivián and Seleme— "and following information coming from trusted sources, including some of the same MNR leaders that denounced me, I knew the revolution was coming but the timing was still unknown. I knew the situation had to be remedied, and the remedy was to have the *junta* call direct elections. This needed to happen within a reasonable period, and the sooner the better."

On December 30, 1951, Ballivián summoned Humbertó, Seleme, and other military and government officials to the Palacio Quemado to attend a cabinet meeting. Ballivián initiated the meeting with a summary of the news. *Ultima Hora*, *La Razon*, and *El Diario*, the three major La Paz newspapers, had reported a pending "violent campaign" against the *junta*.

Once again, Humbertó voiced the urgent need to hold general elections. "In light of the present government's unpopularity, a simple and decisive act of government was required.... I exclaimed there was still time!"

The debate continued for three more months.

"MY INSPIRATION," HUMBERTÓ wrote, "was to find a solution that would benefit all Bolivians; forgetting the game as well as any hatred, grudges or vengeance." While he represented the new government's prodemocracy faction, his opposition is hard to define. A group vehemently opposed to elections, or a block of people who supported maintaining military rule, would have represented a clear rival. These people existed, but they were insignificant in number or otherwise incapable of directing the outcome of the government's predicament. A small faction of opportunistic men were the ones who brought down the *junta*.

From exile in Arequipa, Humbertó concluded Seleme had been "the author of this unparalleled act of vandalism." He was the principle force impeding the electoral processes, and he was the one who had weakened the military's influence and its attempt to direct a peaceful path.

In his manifesto, Humbertó addressed his former colleague: "Seleme, 'minister' of Ballivián's government; Seleme, a man who was 'loyal' to the *junta* and our mission; Seleme, 'prosecutor' of the MNR and of conspiracy; Seleme, the man who accused me of conspiring against Bolivia. In the end, Seleme, Seleme, Seleme. To you, the man who threw away the trust of Ballivián as well as the confidence of your fellow ministers; to you, greedy man who cared only for feeding your own voracious appetite—Seleme you crow!"

CONCERN OVER THE escalating political situation had prevented Humbertó from fulfilling his duty to inspect military garrisons across the country. He devoted the month of February 1952 to this work, visiting Oruro, Cochabamba, Santa Cruz, Roboré and Puerto Suárez. His departure from La Paz opened a door to conspiracy.

"During my absence," Humbertó wrote, "representatives from the MNR reached out to Coronel Edmundo Paz Soldán, the army chief of staff, proposing that he incite a revolution, and then assume the presidency." Paz Soldán, a close colleague and friend of Humbertó's, rejected the offer stating he did not have a reason to take such a serious step. He too was counting on the word of General Ballivián to constitutionalize the country.

While Humbertó was away, Seleme used his position as head of the military police to develop a fighting unit that could counter the army. In secret, he connected with Hernán Siles Zuazo from the MNR, committing his 2,000 person-strong police force to support their cause.

On February 4, Ballivián asked Humbertó and the officers under his command to meet with him at the Palacio Quemado to voice their opinions. As if he was citing witnesses, Humbertó meticulously listed the names of the men who attended this meeting: General Jose Quiroga, Inspector General of the Army; General Francisco Arias, Deputy secretary of National defense; General Jorge Rodríguez, Deputy Secretary of Aeronautics; General Noel Monje, General Staff Director; Colonel Edmundo Paz Soldán, Army Chief of Staff, and Colonel Carlos Suárez Guzmán, Air Force Chief of Staff. The officers unanimously concluded Ballivián should proceed with the immediate call for free and direct elections. To emphasize their point, they wrote and signed a letter with a special recommendation to move forward with a concrete and immediate response.

"At 21:00 hours the same day," Humbertó reported, "I delivered this letter in person to Ballivián's office with the request that he respond immediately." Two hours later, he met with Ballivián.

"Very well!" Ballivián said, "This is my salvation. Now, no one can tell me that I have betrayed the country. Tell the generals I agree and will give you my affirmative answer tomorrow."

It took three more days for Ballivián to supply this answer. He invited Humbertó back to the palace. Humbertó left that meeting believing he had succeeded. He wrote, "the tone of Ballivián's response suggested his support for constitutionalizing the country."

If Ballivián agreed to hold an election, the decision does not appear to have been documented or well-communicated. In the absence of this agreement, throughout the spring of 1952, the revolutionary tension continued to rise.

HUMBERTÓ RECOUNTED HIS experiences from April 9, 1952, day one of the Bolivian Revolution. "Early in the morning, Seleme called me at home to inform me he had just learned the press was preparing to report on the collapse of the *junta*. After confirming he communicated the news was false, Seleme pardoned the inconvenience, and said goodbye."

Despite the mistrust that existed between the two generals, it seems reasonable Humbertó would have accepted Seleme's claim. Accusations and rumors were rampant; a part of the daily experience.

Of course, this time was different. The news reports were accurate. Seleme's call was simply an attempt to distract Humbertó and the military for as long as possible. "From this point," Humbertó added, "Seleme had a few hours to initiate his revolution undisturbed by me while I slept at home."

THE BATTLE FOR La Paz began at 6:15 AM that morning. The military police combined forces with insurgents and targeted military outposts and armaments garrisons in La Paz.

"One shot... Two shots... I could tell the fighting was raging near the barracks of our motorized regiment," Humbertó wrote. "Just before leaving my home, I learned over the radio Seleme had pledged his support to the MNR. I went first to the Ministry of Defense, and then to El Alto which fulfilled plan No. 1 of the nation's defense strategy."

In El Alto, Humbertó learned several of his aides had not reported to their posts. Presumably, they had changed sides. He issued orders to infantry units across the country to come to the aid of La Paz. These soldiers and their equipment would have to travel by land, train or foot, a process that would last many days.

Attempting to calm the situation, Humbertó ordered troops who were already in El Alto to avoid contact with the insurgents. He also tried to initiate negotiations with the MNR. Later, he learned his communications could not be transmitted as the phone lines connecting El Alto with La Paz had been cut.

Humbertó received a report from a battalion commander in La Paz. "Since 16:00 hours, civilian factions have been attacking posts adjacent to the weapons and ammunitions barracks. We have contained these attacks with fire mortars and automatic weapons. Pressure is intense. The fighting is consuming our ammunition. Require additional troops immediately. Requesting an immediate response. "

Humbertó replied, "As of 17:00 hours, except for the Andean-based military units, no other troops have yet arrived."

In the morning of April 10, the revolutionary forces unleashed a major offensive on a La Paz-based battalion. Attempting to elevate the morale of troops fighting in the city, Humbertó ordered an air force attack. More fireworks display than an assault, his planes dropped bombs on targets in sparsely populated areas in the city's higher altitudes.

Around the same time, waves of armed police along with miners equipped with dynamite, which they possessed in abundance as a tool of their trade, ascended to El Alto. They destroyed the military and civilian airports along with armament stockpiles. Humbertó lamented his soldiers' poor preparations. "Our cadets had barely ten weeks of instruction. Our troops had very little combat experience."

Around this time, insurgents began to attack military bases in

El Alto and Viacha, a town located a few miles to the southwest of the city. "I was informed the insurgents were in possession of my location and were planning to capture me. For this reason, I decided to move to Guaqui," a town and military base located at the southern tip of Lake Titicaca.

By the end of the day, army units around El Alto, Viacha and Guaqui had begun to collapse. Miners attacked other units traveling from Oruro, Challapata, Curahuara de Corangas and other towns throughout the Altiplano as they attempted to reach La Paz.

AT 8:00 AM on Friday, April 11, 1952, Humbertó received a radio transmission from Hernán Siles Zuazo who requested a meeting to discuss the definitive end of hostilities.

Humbertó wrote, "I chose the village of Laja" (fifteen miles from La Paz) "for this meeting. I was joined by Dr. Siles Zuazo along with Colonel Edmundo Paz Soldán, Major Emilio Molína Pizarro, Jorge del Solar, Eduardo Rioja Pelaéz, Fulvio Ballón, Generals Francisco Arias and Jorge Rodríguez, and Colonel Claudio Moreno. In the presence of these men, I signed the petition for the immediate cessation of fire. There was no capitulation by any side."

Humbertó also noted, "In the course of thirty-two years, Bolivia has confronted more than thirty revolutionary events. None of these prospered. As I understand, an internal shock can never bring healthy effects. Still, it made sense to stop the fighting, and begin to progress the country."

It deserves mention, despite Humbertó's misgivings, the group of men he handed the government over to stayed in power for the next twelve years.

Upon returning to Guaqui, Humbertó requested immediate retirement from active duty. Soon afterward, he learned of the arrest of military officers in La Paz. "These were men who did nothing but conform to their duty, and obey orders from their superiors," he wrote. On April 13, Humbertó met with Colonel Paz Soldán, his friend and confidant who the MNR had recently offered the presidency to. To help ensure Humbertó's safety, Paz Soldán directed him to the border town of Desaguadero to seek asylum in Peru. A few days later, Humbertó arrived in Arequipa.

On April 18, Humbertó received a telegram requesting his return to Bolivia to stand trial for his role in provoking the revolution. He declined to participate.

TOWARD THE END of the manifesto, Humbertó declared, "As for other versions circulating about my person, it is absolutely false that I participated in or had any knowledge of any revolutionary plan. The attack by the police force on the army barracks was not an isolated act. On the contrary, this was an action derived from a long-term plan led by communists and directed toward a specific objective: to destroy the armed forces, which was solidly united in its role to service all the people of Bolivia.

"The conduct of the army was framed by constitutional rules, laws and regulations.... If the army had not acted as it did, it would have abandoned its role and become an element of disorder.... History will judge our actions. We were all united by our duty as soldiers to the fatherland. The Bolivian blood poured in the revolution originated from the first shot from a bad man who assaulted our military arsenals to arm the insurgents."

He closed, "My dear, loyal and noble comrades, heroic cadets from the military academy —who were always the pride and hope of the fatherland—officers and soldiers of the army of Bolivia, hold your heads high and proud. Join me in exclaiming the historic phrase that we will make our own, 'Everything has been lost but our honor.' Signed, Arequipa, Peru, May 9, 1952. General Humbertó Torres Ortíz."

DURING THE YEAR he was in power, Humbertó displayed admirable qualities. He was loyal and trustworthy. He felt he was doing right for the people of Bolivia. Despite these qualities, it is hard to overlook how his calls for new elections ignored the fact these people had already voted in favor of the MNR.

Ballivián's indecision reflected the frustratingly slow pace, and often excessive formality of Bolivian politics, and perhaps global politics overall. He made many false or nebulous commitments— assurances progress would happen *manaña*, which in Bolivia means it could happen, or maybe not; perhaps tomorrow, perhaps not.

It is likely the adversaries of the military *junta* felt they too were on righteous paths. Paz Estenssoro, Siles Zuazo, and the other founders of the MNR, likely believed their mission was to improve the quality of life of their constituents.

Conceivably, even Seleme felt he was pursuing a noble vision. And yet, he must have considered the likeliness of negative consequences resulting from his schemes. It is hard to forgive politicians of such sizable missteps.

Whatever the outcome of the debate around who was right and who was wrong, it remains clear the Bolivian National Revolution of 1952, which is also known as the Bolivian Agrarian Revolution, was the country's most significant political event of the twentieth century. The revolution was unprecedented but not unwarranted. It is a tale of a group of powerful men who failed to pay enough attention to the transformations taking place in their society. It is a story of broken allegiances, unkept promises and failed attempts to hold onto antiquated practices and policies. This is an aging history, but also a contemporary account. The back and forth nature of Bolivian politics—broad swings from the right to the left and back again—continued through the end of the twentieth century. There are indications these shifts could return.

ONE YEAR AFTER Humbertó fled Bolivia, Alicia and their three children joined him in Peru. Silvya was sixteen years old. "We had very little money," she said. "No possessions. Just ourselves. But with the help of a few people, we made it work. We moved into a tiny apartment. There was one small bathroom. A little patio with a room where we prepared our meals, and a washbasin for our laundry."

The family rented their apartment from a couple who Silvya addressed as Don and Doña Cucalón. This formal description conceals deep sentiments of respect and gratitude. At the time when Silvya's family most needed assistance, this man and woman had stepped up to help.

"They knew a little about my father, and they knew we were refugees," Silvya said. "Doña Cucalón would regularly bring my mother big pots of soup. She never asked for payment." Favors like these enabled the family to survive.

Their apartment was located a few blocks from Arequipa's downtown. The family could access the rooftop of their apartment building. From there, they had a full view of the city and the surrounding environment. There was the Misti Volcano, snowcapped and steaming. As in La Paz and Turin, Arequipa had a massive and omnipresent mountain-protector.

It was a hard time, but it created some positive memories. The event that tore the family apart also brought them and their community closer together. "Because much of the Bolivian Army was in exile," Silvya said, "there were many Bolivians living in Arequipa. My brother, sister and I became friends with many of the cadets. I remember Carnival and dancing. I remember sneaking cigarettes from my parents and smoking them with my siblings and our friends."

At night from their rooftop, Humbertó and his children would stargaze. "It seemed we could see the whole universe," Silvya said. "I'd ask my father hard questions—*Who is up there? Why are we here?*"

"Some people believe we are created by God," he replied. "When we die, we go to another place. Others believe creation is natural. Who knows which is true? But these are the right questions. Curiosity is important. The answers are less meaningful."

CHAPTER 14
Aftermath

El Valle de las Animas, Zona Sur, La Paz, 1996

*"The life of the dead is placed in
the memory of the living."*

—CICERO

T HE LA PAZ Cemetery covers two-square miles, or fifteen city
blocks, on the slopes climbing from La Paz to El Alto. Com-
muters and travelers know the surrounding neighborhood as a
bustling transportation center. *Trufi* drivers—operators of the ubiquitous La Paz minivans—launch their routes from the avenues and
plazas adjoining the cemetery. This network then crisscrosses the
city, extending throughout the Altiplano, and off to the Chilean and
Peruvian borders.

Before the cemetery existed, deceased Paceños and Paceñas had
been laid to rest underneath or around the city's churches and public
buildings. As the population grew, this became impractical. In 1826,
civic planners established the cemetery as a long-term solution to the
city's growth challenges.

In the 1930s, the Bolivian government took control of the cemetery, and committed to administer it in service of the city's needier
residents. To manage available space, the government introduced a
policy allowing people to rent crypt spaces for up to ten years. At the
end of this period, families of the deceased were to receive options.

They could move the remains of their loved ones to alternative burial sites outside of the cemetery, or they could move them to smaller crypts within it.

Colorful yet modest, these petite crypts are often adorned with flowers and photos of the deceased. Perhaps as a reflection of their inhabitant's former personalities, many of these plots have façades painted with flashes of bright pink, blue, or yellow. Stacks upon stacks, the rectangular-shaped crypts aggregate to create multistory mausoleums. These resemble apartment buildings, or micro-housing, for the dead.

The mausoleums are set in a grid suggesting planned urban design. These are places of celebration and ritual. On special days— *El Día de las Ñatitas*, for example—the cemetery hums. Festivities often extend beyond the cemetery, into streets and homes throughout the city. Outsiders, including tourists, are welcome to stop by to share a drink or a bite to eat. Moments of celebration and remembrance also serve notice, time passes for all of us, even the most spirited and virtuous.

IN 1957, ALICIA's father, Crisologo, fell ill. The revolutionaries had forced his daughter, son-in-law and grandchildren into exile. The government, fueled by new agrarian reform laws, had confiscated the bulk of his beloved *finca*. This shifting world conspired with old age to impair his health.

Five years had passed since the war. Alicia and her children now had the option to return to Bolivia without fear of retribution from the government. With the MNR still in power, Humbertó's options remained limited.

Silvya's brother, Beto, was midway through his high school studies. He was focused on securing admission to an architecture program at a university in Argentina. Staying in school in Peru maximized his prospects for academic success. Recognizing this, Humbertó decided to remain in Arequipa with his son.

Alicia needed to attend to her father, and so in 1958, she returned to La Paz with Gloria and Silvya at her side. Shortly after they returned, Crisologo passed away, at peace in the sunroom of his home on *calle* Ingavi.

"I remember my grandfather's funeral and the sadness I felt," Silvya said. "I also remember going to movies and on walks with my friends. It was nice to be back in Bolivia."

Ordinary circumstances—death with life, and grief with happiness.

AROUND THE SAME time, the MNR's revolutionary vision and socialist policies started to lose some of their shine. Waxing then waning, the Bolivian political scene began to resettle along a time-established sequence. The longer left-leaning politicians remained in power, the higher the likelihood conservatists would return.

As a humanitarian gesture and reconciliatory motion designed to bridge the chasm separating the MNR from its adversaries, then President Hernán Siles Zuazo began to issue pardons to the militarists from 1952. Humbertó received one of these. He was now welcome to return home.

In 1960, Beto left Peru to attend university in Salta, Argentina. This allowed Humbertó to join Alicia and their girls who had relocated back to Cochabamba. They selected this city because they had family there. They also knew Humbertó would be able to find work. He was well-known and well-liked. People in Cochabamba, and elsewhere in the Bolivian lowlands, were more inclined to agree with his ideologies, or the ones characterized by the political establishment he once represented.

"Pablo Gutiérrez, a wealthy cattle rancher hired my father," Silvya said. "He knew my father could organize large groups of people to get things done." Of course, it was also helpful to have the former *commandante general* working at his side.

For the next few years, Humbertó dedicated himself to his new employment. He and his family began to rebuild. They reconnected with their community and the new Bolivia. The environment helped—Cochabamba with its everlasting spring. The family absorbed it all—long walks each day along the city's Avenida del Prado; taking in the trees and flowers; eating ice creams on Saturdays.

ONE DAY, WHILE riding as a passenger in the back seat of her car, Alicia was involved in an accident. Her driver crashed their Volkswagen Beetle into the rear end of another vehicle. At that time, use of seatbelts was not common. The collision dislodged Alicia from the back of the car. She flew forward and hit her head on the inside of the car's windshield. Thankful for having avoided more serious injuries, she returned home holding a bandage to her head and complaining of a light headache.

It is unclear if it was the car crash or some other underlying condition that initiated her decline. Nonetheless, Alicia was never the same after the accident. Additional symptoms appeared—sluggishness, dizzy spells, and confusion. A few months after the crash, she returned to the hospital expecting to have a short visit. Her doctors discovered she had suffered a stroke.

Humbertó, their children, and other family members gathered at the hospital to hold vigil and pray. Alicia slipped into a coma. She never came out.

It all happened fast.

Humbertó gave the physicians permission to remove the tubes from his wife's body. In November 1963, the week after John F. Kennedy's assassination, Alicia passed away at age sixty-one.

Silvya recalled, "The morning she died, I walked home from the hospital. When I arrived, I saw the lady who lived with us preparing our living room for the wake. At that time, there were no funeral homes. Our custom was to hold the service at home."

The family placed Alicia's body on display for one day. Afterward, they buried her in the Sanjinés's family tomb at the La Paz Cemetery.

"At that time, children were more protected. Our parents did not discuss their feelings with us," Silvya said. "But we could feel it. I could feel it. Losing my mother was very hard, especially for my father. The loss destroyed him."

ONE YEAR BEFORE Alicia passed away, Humbertó met a young man named Joseph DeSousa. He was among the first of group of North Americans to join the Peace Corps. Inaugurated one year before, the organization had begun to place volunteers in Bolivia, as well as Chile, Ghana, India, and more than twenty other developing countries.

The son of South American immigrants of Portuguese ancestry, and the youngest of eleven children, Joe, as he was known, was born in Brooklyn, New York in 1931. He grew up in the working class Bensonhurst neighborhood during the Great Depression. Overcoming setbacks, he had served in the US Army before earning a bachelor's degree in economics from Hofstra University, and then a master's degree from Rutgers University.

In the Peace Corps, Joe volunteered as an economics professor at the Universidad de San Andrés, Bolivia's leading public university. When he first met Humbertó, Joe had been dating one of Silvya's cousins, Rosario, who worked at the US Embassy in La Paz. Humbertó offered to rent him the family's home in La Paz. The arrangement worked for both. Humbertó had someone to look after the house while the family lived in Cochabamba, and Joe had access to Humbertó.

Joe would frequently travel six hours—maybe ten depending on the road conditions—by bus from La Paz to Cochabamba to meet with Humbertó. Perhaps apartment-related topics were a suitable excuse for the visits. Possibly, Joe just wanted to spend time with Humbertó. After all, Joe was an economist, and fond of history. Humbertó had played a principal role defining his country's contemporary story.

There may have been other reasons for the visits.

Looking past the detail he was dating her cousin, Joe grew increasingly fond of Silvya. In turn, she became fond of him. "He was smart," she later said, "always a source of insight and thoughtful comments."

Silvya was in her twenties at that time. To her, this young American man represented adventure. He offered her a path to a new life at a time when doors appeared to be closing. It was not love at first sight, but the best option given the circumstances.

WHILE LIVING IN Arequipa, Humbertó had been diagnosed with prostate cancer. For several years, his symptoms remained under control. Losing his wife, however, seemed to revive the disease. As had occurred with Alicia, illness drove Humbertó's rapid deterioration. In November 1965, at the age of sixty-three, he passed away. "Even though his cancer had returned," Silvya said, "I know he died from a broken heart."

In death, Humbertó received the tributes that eluded him in life. He was awarded a military memorial in Cochabamba. Afterward, his body was flown to La Paz for a second military procession. A soldier who served under his command in Roboré volunteered for the duty to pilot the plane carrying his casket. For one day, his body was placed on display at the Bolivian Military Club in the Plaza Murillo. Then, Humbertó Torres Ortíz—decorated army captain from the Chaco War, commander of the Bolivian military academy, *commandante general* of the Republic of Bolivia, loving husband and father—was laid to rest in the La Paz Cemetery.

WEIGHING HER OPTIONS, Silvya agreed to Joe's marriage proposal. After a brief engagement, and one month after Humbertó's death, they married in La Paz in December 1965. Silvya had mixed feelings about her relationship with Joe. She was attracted to his intellect and charm, but also observed his strong opinions and short temper. Alice—Silvya and Joe's daughter and my wife—summarized, "She found him intelligent. She didn't speak any English, but she had always wanted to travel and live overseas. Marrying my dad made this possible."

Joe completed his Peace Corps service and returned to Washington D.C. alone. Back in the US, he secured a job with the US Agency for International Development. A few months later, he was back in La Paz working and living with Silvya.

Their first child, Richard, was born shortly after. A year later, the new family moved to Bloomington, Indiana where Joe began a PhD program in economics at Indiana University. This return to academia provided a window into Joe's tumultuous and inconsistent personality. He never completed his coursework. "He thought it was stupid," Silvya said with a laugh. "He thought he knew more than his professors."

Joe quit the program, received a new job with the US State Department, and moved with Silvya and Richard to Bogota, Colombia where their second child, Robert, was born. Pursuing the diplomat's lifestyle, a few years later, they were off to Addis Ababa, Ethiopia where Alice was born. Four years after that, in 1975, they landed, more permanently this time, in McLean, Virginia where Silvya began her life in the suburbs. A regular woman with an irregular story, her atypical past became concealed by her ordinary surroundings.

TEN YEARS AFTER Humbertó's death, Silvya returned to La Paz to visit his grave. "I didn't like how his body was separated from my mother's body," she said, "so I asked my brother to help me move him into our grandfather's crypt." While Beto agreed to take her to the La Paz Cemetery, moving the body was to be her undertaking. "I guess I am very brave, so I agreed to do it," she said.

"When I first saw his body, I received a shock. A strong feeling of lament, which was deeper than a cry and something I had never experienced, took over me. I wrapped his remains in a shawl, which was the custom in my country. The one I had wasn't big enough, so I had to go buy another one."

Stores and kiosks selling flowers along with other funerary items and services line the streets surrounding the La Paz Cemetery. With her brother standing close by, Silvya left to find a larger "holy sheet," as she called the cloth. Outside of the cemetery, her walk escalated to a run, and tears began streaming down her face.

"I was crying, sobbing really, so aggressively I couldn't stop." Decades of bottled emotions escaped her. Both of her parents had died much earlier than expected. She now lived in a distant and unfamiliar country, far removed from her family, friends, and the environment she treasured.

It wasn't supposed to turn out this way.

Silvya couldn't just run away. She purchased the shawl and returned to the cemetery. After carefully wrapping her father's body, she placed it next to her mother's body, and close to Crisologo and other deceased family members. Humbertó could now rest where he would have wanted to.

The following pages feature a selection of images of Humbertó, Alicia, Crisologo, Silvya and others. They depict scenes from Bolivia, Italy and Chile. Except when noted, the image creator is unknown.

"Humbertó Torres Ortíz and Alicia Sanjinés Vidaurre," by Alice DeSousa Stewart

*In the Yungas, date unknown, including Mama Carmen and Crisologo,
back row, right-hand side; Alicia front row, first from left.*

La Paz 1° de Diciembre de 1928

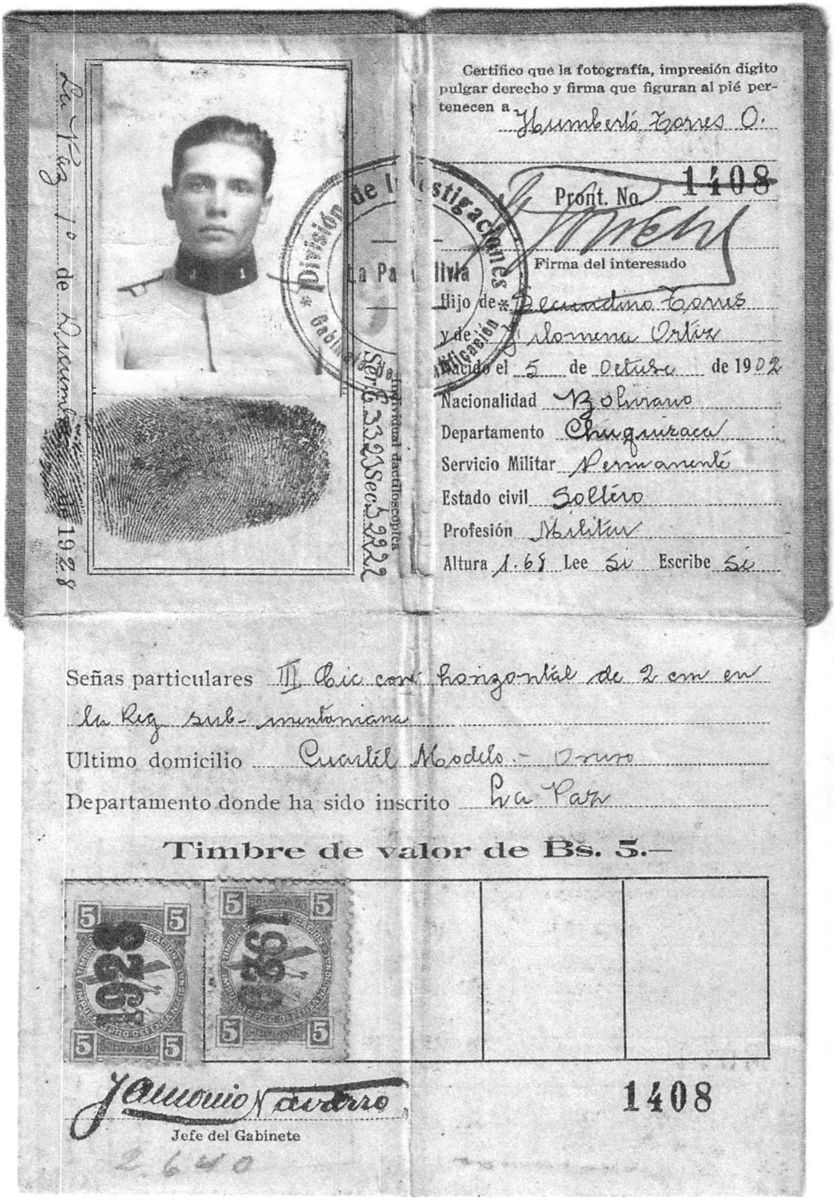

Certifico que la fotografía, impresión digito pulgar derecho y firma que figuran al pié pertenecen a Humbertó Torres O.

Pront. No 1408

Firma del interesado

División de Investigaciones
La Paz — Bolivia
Gabinete de Identificación

Individual dactiloscópica
Ser. E 3323 Sec. S 2222

Hijo de Bernardino Torres
y de Filomena Ortiz
Nacido el 5 de Octubre de 1902
Nacionalidad Boliviano
Departamento Chuquisaca
Servicio Militar Permanente
Estado civil Soltero
Profesión Militar
Altura 1.69 Lee Si Escribe Si

Señas particulares III Cic con horizontal de 2 cm en la Reg. sub-mentoniana
Ultimo domicilio Cuartel Modelo - Oruro
Departamento donde ha sido inscrito La Paz

Timbre de valor de Bs. 5.—

5 5 5 5
1928

Jancovio Navarro
Jefe del Gabinete

1408

2640

Humbertó Torres Ortíz personal identity card, La Paz, December 1, 1928

ABOVE: *First from left — Humbertó in Italy, circa 1939*

BELOW: *Second from right — Humbertó in Italy, circa 1939*

ABOVE: *Front row center — Humbertó, Comandante*
of the Escuala de Armas, Cochabamba 1944

BELOW: *Second from right – Humbertó and Alicia,*
Bolivian Military Attaché to Chile, circa 1948

ABOVE: *On left, in uniform — Humbertó in Roboré, circa 1950*

BELOW: *Junta Militar – Humbertó, front row, second from left, with Ballivián, front row center, 1951. Seleme not pictured.*

Military Funeral — General Humbertó Torres Ortíz,
Cochabamba, November 1965

"Silvya Gladys Angelica Torres Sanjinés"
by Alice DeSousa Stewart

IN THE MID-1960S, around the time of Humbertó's death, a new band of revolutionaries moved to Bolivia. These people included a middle-aged Argentinian doctor who arrived in La Paz in 1966 posing as an Uruguayan businessman. A decade before, he had helped topple the government of Fulgencio Batista in Cuba. Pursuing the vision of a unified South America and understanding achieving this goal required igniting the spirit of the indigenous peoples, this doctor, Ernesto "Che" Guevara, selected Bolivia as the launching pad for a global socialist crusade.

Che and his men moved south, to the Chaco. There they became bogged down by many of the same elements Humbertó had faced during the war with Paraguay three decades earlier. Harassed by heat, disease, and insects, the band moved north.

The US government ascertained their plans and sent operatives to assist the Bolivian Army in capturing Che and his comrades. In October 1967, the rebels were apprehended in the town of La Higuera in the department of Santa Cruz. Promised a court-martial, Che was then brought to the nearby town of Vallegrande. The next day, he was shot and killed.

"He was executed, that was reprehensible. But you must

Street art in Copacabana, 2011

think about things at the moment that they happened. In that moment, it was justified," Gary Prado, the soldier who caught him, later said. (Laurence Blair 2017)

As Che and his men marched through Bolivia, a different group of foreign rebels made their way to South America. Distancing themselves from their pasts, they worked to blend into communities across the continent. When it served them, they contributed to local efforts to drive populist and military agendas.

One of these men arrived under the alias, Klaus Altmann. He was a former German military officer. At the end of the Second World War, US intelligence officers had captured him. Instead of imprisoning him, they put him to work as an agent in the expanding Cold War. Years later, sensing the expansion of a communist agenda in South America—the same movement that attracted Che Guevara to the continent—the US sent Altmann to Bolivia to observe and assist the anti-communist movement.

During the Second World War, this same man had served as the Gestapo chief in Lyon, France. The Nazis appointed him to this post to eradicate the French Resistance. He was largely successful, to the point his given name drew reactions of hatred and fear from the people he persecuted. He was Nikolaus "Klaus" Barbie, The Butcher of Lyon.

Splitting time between Bolivia and Peru, Barbie lived comfortably. During the early 1970s, he had raised funds for the Bolivian president, a dictator and former general named Hugo Banzer Suárez, to purchase the armaments he required for a successful coup. For his service, friendship, and expertise, the Banzer-led government appointed Barbie to the rank of Lt. Colonel in the Bolivian armed forces.

While in La Paz, Barbie had a reliable routine which included passing time in his favorite café, the Confitería Club de La Paz, on the Avenida Mariscal Santa Cruz not far from the Plaza Murillo. In recognition of his former patronage, during my time in Bolivia, the café was known by tourists simply as the Nazi Café. A place worthy of a visit, it retained a décor first placed there a half-a-century before—simple yet comfortable; wooden and smoky.

Barbie claimed his role in France was an honorable one, dedicated to the service of his country during its time of need. After all, he was just acting on orders delivered to him by his superiors. He also believed the passing of decades distanced him from anything bad he might have done. It was time the world moved on.

The French and Israeli Nazi hunters who pursued him disagreed. They knew Barbie as a shrewd, calculated, and sadistic torturer and murder of thousands of people—political activists and students; men, women and children. The Nazi hunters included men like Régis Debray. In 1967, the Bolivian military had captured Debray with Che Guevara in La Higuera and sentenced him to thirty years in prison. Bolivia released Debray from prison in 1970. In the 1980s, he served as an assistant to President Francois Mitterand. Under Mitterand, French authorities tasked him with the kidnapping of Barbie, who they believed was living in Bolivia. Another shift in Bolivian politics, from socialist to conservative rule, opened the door to less dramatic tactics.

In the end, the Bolivian government under President Hernán Siles Zuazo, who was serving his second term, nabbed Barbie for tax evasion. Bolivian police arrested Barbie in La Paz and stripped him of his Bolivian citizenship for lying about his role with the Nazis. In

1983, Bolivia extradited Barbie to France. Four years later, a French court convicted him of crimes against humanity and sentenced him to life in prison. He died of leukemia in a French jail in 1991.

HUMBERTÓ TORRES ORTÍZ, Víctor Paz Estenssoro, Che Guevara, and Klaus Barbie, contemporaries with diverse backgrounds, personalities and objectives. Some were bad people who did horrific things. Others were good people who made bad decisions. While their stories are an aging history, they remain central to the contemporary Bolivian narrative, and a reflection of the complexity of Bolivian culture and politics.

CHAPTER 15

The Peace Corps

Chacaltaya Ski Area, 1997

"Peace requires the simple but powerful recognition that what we have in common as human beings is more important and crucial than what divides us."

—SARGENT SHRIVER, 1ST DIRECTOR OF
THE PEACE CORPS, 1961–1966

JUST SHY OF 18,000 feet above sea level, Mt. Chacaltaya is, or was, the home of the world's highest lift-served ski area. While no one disputes the altitude, the association between Chacaltaya, skiing, and snow had long been exaggerated.

This "ski area" supported a single run. The loan "ski lift": a rope tow-type mechanical contraption that stitched together cables extending from the bottom to the top of a glacier-wrapped Andean pitch. The cables then rerouted across a gorge to the top of the mountain where they passed into a clapboard shack.

Within this structure, an antique truck placed on blocks replaced conventional ski lift instrumentation. Entering from a hole in the wall, the cables then passed under the hood of this automobile. There they circled around and around, from pulley to pulley, gaining power before reversing course, back out of the building, across the gorge, and down the mountain linking each of the rope tow towers.

Chug, chug, that old engine delivered just enough power to drive the lift.... Just enough power, or several times each day, not quite enough. A standard experience in many corners of this laid-back *mañana culture*, the engine might just stop running, for a few minutes, or for the rest of the day.

Alpinists did not head to Chacaltaya expecting world-class skiing. The uniqueness of the experience tied to the location. The "world's highest" designation justified the attempt to visit it.

Founded in 1939, this was among South America's first ski areas. Chug, chug, the activity stopped in 2010 when the glacier, which had existed for twenty thousand years, dissolved, a casualty of global warming.

Bolivia delivers adventure coupled with life at a slower pace. These benefits are balanced by change at the mercy of many forces, all mightier than the country.

WITH UNDEVELOPED SKILLS, and without knowing much about what to expect, I went to Bolivia in search of uncommon experiences including those obtainable in the Cordillera Real and in the jungles of the Amazon basin.

My experience began a few weeks after I graduated college. I flew to Miami to join thirty other fresh Peace Corps recruits in a short pre-voyage training conducted at a hotel on Miami Beach. Despite the more than comfortable location, a wave of anxiety hit me as I drove to the hotel. I was embarking on a two-year expedition to an obscure country without knowing anyone. Just as easily as it arrived, this stress dissolved. I discovered those thirty other recruits were in a similar space.

My cohort of volunteers included Mary, a two-time Olympian, Mike, a former Washington Post sportswriter, and Bruce, a true man of mystery who joined the Peace Corps after spending thirty years in a ten-family village in Alaska, north of the Arctic Circle.

Accomplished professionals joined people like me—young adults, just out of college, and eager to take on our first career challenge. We mixed with others who moved to Bolivia attempting to hit reset after unsatisfying jobs or failed marriages. Despite our varied backgrounds, we were unified in our decision to take the leap and place ourselves in an entirely unfamiliar environment. This attribute surpassed all others and became the one that bonded our friendship.

WITH AN EXECUTIVE Order, John F. Kennedy established the Peace Corps in 1961. He founded the program to provide social and economic assistance and promote a mutual understanding between citizens of the US and citizens of the countries served by the Peace Corps. Since the program's inception, more than two hundred thousand people have volunteered in one hundred forty countries, including all South American nations apart from French Guiana.

A component of the US government's annual foreign aid budget, the Peace Corps relies on congressional support. The organization consistently receives funding, in my view, not due to altruism, but because it is a low-cost way to expand influence of the United States abroad. The Peace Corps is an economic and social counterbalance to US military presence overseas, and a nonviolent way for citizens to express patriotism.

Politics have always influenced the program. Initial opponents included Richard Nixon who disliked the Peace Corps because he predicted it would become a vessel for draft dodgers trying to escape the Vietnam War. While domestic sentiment has improved, perceptions abroad continue to fluctuate.

Bolivia was one of the first countries served by the Peace Corps. The first volunteers—including Joseph DeSousa—arrived in 1962. Toward the end of that decade, the Bolivian film, *Yawar Mallku*, or *Blood of the Condor*, portrayed volunteers as a partying band of gringo misfits on a mission to sterilize locals. This depiction was largely untrue. Nonetheless, Bolivian politicians exploited the film as if it were a documentary. In 1971, Bolivia asked the Peace Corps—which exists in countries on the invitation of the local governments—to leave.

Relations with the US slowly improved. In the early 1990s, Bolivia invited the Peace Corps back. Two groups of approximately thirty volunteers deployed to the country each year. My group, Bolivia 14, arrived in May 1996.

After two days in Miami, we entered a two-month cultural, language, and vocational immersion program near Sacaba, a village outside of Cochabamba. Each day, our instructors corralled my group of aspiring volunteers inside a walled compound. To outsiders, our presence may have echoed some of the sequences from *Blood of the Condor*—a few dozen loud and awkward Americans locked inside an enigmatic, gated facility.

The activities taking place inside were nonthreatening. We fumbled with our Quechua, Aymara or Guarani lessons. These are Bolivia's three primary indigenous languages. They feature explosive sounds or nasalized vowels. The grammar and pronunciation were incomparable to anything we had read, spoken or heard before.

We learned practical skills including how to build an outhouse, and which crops are easiest to grow. (Radishes!) We studied local cultural and business norms, as well as how to adjust to the anticipated shock of feeling jettisoned from our homes, families, and friends.

During the immersion program, I rented a room from an indigenous and evangelical Christian family who lived in a compound in the nearby village of Entre Ríos. Their standard of living appeared to resemble that of the other people from their community. They had intermittent access to electricity—lights on during the evening, and off during the day. Water came from a well which had been dug beneath a patio in the front of their compound. All family members and their guests used a latrine. Nothing more than a hole without walls, this was located toward the back of the compound.

The family was kind to me, yet my connection with them was transactional. They wanted additional income. My employer and the source of my rent was a safe bet. One of the few meals I shared with them resulted in my first of what would become many bouts with dysentery. While serving me a bowl of rice, the mother of the family used her hands as serving spoons. Despite having just received instruction on the basics of food hygiene—including an introduction to the dangers and prevalence of something descriptively called *the fecal-oral cycle,* and ignoring the knowledge that this family did not have access to running water or proper sanitation—I graciously accepted her food offering.

Adjusting to different foods as well as distinct bacteria is a standard, initial step for anyone moving across continents. The rice and potato-rich Andean diet coupled with a series of stomach ailments led me to drop thirty pounds in my first two months in the country. Under certain circumstances, I might have welcomed this. At six feet tall and having fallen to an exceedingly slim one hundred forty pounds, I was beginning to dwindle away. Fantasy imaginings of bonding with the locals now dispelled, for the duration of my Peace Corps training, I opted to take my meals out.

During the day, I attempted to bulk up on calories at the Peace Corps training compound. At night, I'd join other volunteers for dinner in Cochabamba. We got to know the restaurants and bars situated along or close to the city's main avenue, the Prado, which was where Silvya and her family had once enjoyed long leisurely strolls. Restaurant Metropolis, well-loved by Peace Corps volunteers for its large plates of spaghetti, became a favorite. We also went to Baubi's restaurant. The fading shadow of the letter "m" on the sign outside the restaurant revealed it had once been called Bambi's. Due to copyright infringement, an essentially alien concept in Bolivia, the owners were somehow compelled to make the slight branding adjustment. Nevertheless, the sign adorning the entrance to the restaurant retained the familiar cartoon imagery borrowed from Disney.

While Cochabamba is logged in my mind as a generally undistinguished place, it is also the location of my most important Peace Corps experience. One year into my service, I met Alice there. The moment I saw her, ascending the spiral staircase in my friend Patrick's squalid Cochabamba apartment, I knew she was the one. After meeting her, I too would search for excuses to take a bus six, or maybe ten hours from La Paz to Cochabamba to see her. Because of this, Cochabamba forever has a place in my heart.

WHILE OTHER PEACE Corps milestones happened in or around that city, most of my experiences occurred elsewhere, including in La Paz which is where I lived for most of my service. Despite Peace

Corp Bolivia's preference to place volunteers in rural locations, I landed a role in the city. I joined a team of Bolivians and Germans working with an organization called INFOCAL, Instituto Nacional de Formación y Capacitación Laboral, which was the equivalent of a technical college. Our multi-year project focused on helping laborers who wanted to transition from their jobs as miners or unskilled manual laborers to more viable forms of employment.

My role was to create a business training course featuring the basic elements of accounting, administration, and marketing. As I had just completed my undergraduate studies, my contributions were commensurate with my age and experience. To build a curriculum that had any semblance of usefulness for our target audience, I had to meet with these people. I had to experience a touch of their reality.

My INFOCAL colleagues and I focused our attention on the underdeveloped and underserved towns surrounding the country's seven principal cities: La Paz-El Alto, Santa Cruz, Sucre, Cochabamba, Potosí, Oruro, and Tarija. The project brought me to all these places, and their surrounding environs.

Throughout my time in Bolivia, I adopted a favorable interpretation of the local work-ethic, convincing myself twenty-hours of light labor each week was aligned with the cultural norm. While it seems accurate to suggest most Bolivians are less adherent to the stressful and strict work standards of their developed world counterparts, my work schedule reflected a desire to live a free-form lifestyle. I was more interested in spending time with my friends and traveling than I was working in an office. I became more proficient at observing the society than contributing to it in any meaningful way.

I spent my days in towns like El Alto seeking to connect with local business owners. I walked the streets armed with a list of business names and addresses. Many of the streets shared the same name. The business owners appeared to have selected their addresses based on personal preferences instead of the arithmetic sequencing mandated by the municipality. This made it difficult to find a specific location. One *Calle* Pucara might intersect with another street of the same name. The building marked *Calle* Pucara No. 2 might be in between the shop at *Calle* Pucara No. 16 and *Calle* Pucara No. 33. The place I was attempting to locate, say the business at *Calle* Pucara No. 4, might exist in a completely different part of town.

I did not always find my destination, but I did meet with many shop owners, mechanics, carpenters, and others who had found a way to establish viable businesses. Like an invited voyeur, I listened to them, took photos, and captured just a taste of their realities.

BEYOND BOLIVIA'S URBAN areas, my job brought me to seldom-visited places. These included Llica, a village near the Chilean border on the edge of the world's largest salt flat. Formed in prehistoric times after ancient salt lakes evaporated, the Salar de Uyuni remains a snow-white, ocean-like expanse. It is set at 11,995 feet above sea level and consumes 4,086 square miles. Llica is two hundred miles, or six hours—maybe twelve depending on the quality of vehicle and the time of year—directly opposite the popular tourist town of Uyuni.

Engaged in a rudimentary attempt to assess Llica's potential for ecotourism, I spent a week there exploring the environment and meeting with villagers. Back then, ecotourism was a novel concept. This model has since become so overpromised it has almost become cliché. Despite this, Bolivia was, and remains, a classic case study.

Cactus bloom in Llica, 1997

The goal of ecotourism is to generate at least the same amount of economic benefit from maintaining a pristine environment as would be gained from exploiting it. I gained my limited knowledge of the subject from a college economics course coupled with a touch of intuition. It became apparent to me, while challenging to reach, Llica had a few things going for it including location and history.

A year and a half in Bolivia had coarsened me to demanding lifestyles. When I traveled in the Altiplano, I anticipated residents could be as cold as their surroundings. The community of Llica surprised me. My accommodations were simple but comfortable. If I needed help, a villager was there to provide it, and for two Bolivianos—about $.25—I treated myself to one of the best showers in recent memory.

A local guide, unexpectedly named Franz, introduced me to some of the *chulpas*, the small stone mausoleums, that mark the surrounding countryside. Untouched for centuries, bits of pottery and ancient tools still littered the ground adjacent to these burial sites.

Franz directed me to one of these graves. Gently removing a few rocks, I peered inside at the mummified remains of a body. It had been placed in a large clay pot. Sitting upright, with knees curled to chest, and arms wrapped around the legs, bits of flesh, hair, and an alpaca shawl still covered it. The body had been preserved in perpetuity by the dry air and abundant minerals surrounding it.

Franz also explained how a recent spate of tomb raiding had increased concerns among the villagers. They were looking for a way to protect and promote their cultural heritage without taking advantage of it. The *chulpas* and their contents—the mummies, pottery, and *aguayo* textiles—could conceivably become a centerpiece in any natural history museum. I didn't have the knowledge or skill required to make any meaningful contribution to Franz's mission. I shouldn't have been allowed to see or touch the ancient artifacts surrounding Llica. Yet there they were, unguarded. There I was, untethered.

At the end of my week in Llica, I caught a ride across the *salar* to the town of Uyuni. Unfortunately, but not unexpectedly, our truck broke down midway. The radiator had developed a hole the size of a silver dollar. Hot steam spewed out of it. By the standards of the developed world, the radiator was unfixable—might as well throw it away and go purchase a new one. We were stranded in the middle of the salt flat with the closest mechanic several hours away. Unfortunate but not unexpected situations like these happen all the time in Bolivia and should be considered part of the experience. Bake them into your plans.

I waited with the other passengers for a fix. Hiding from the sun—with sunrays that scorch and blind you due to the altitude and surrounding endless sea of white—we crouched down on the shady side of the vehicle. Relief came a few hours later. No tow

Breakdown on the Salar de Uyuni, 1997

truck pulled up to solve things. No one airlifted us to safety. The fix happened thanks to our driver's mechanical skills, and necessity. The truck was his livelihood, and the passengers needed to get to their destination.

More than twenty years have passed since I visited the Salar de Uyuni. I don't suspect much has changed. A light form of ecotourism, which is more tourism and less eco, continues to thrive in the bustling and dusty town of Uyuni. The concept and its financial benefits likely never found their way to Llica. I wonder if that town's treasures remain intact and untarnished.

CLOSER TO LA PAZ, I regularly worked in villages along the shores of Lake Titicaca. These included Tiquiña which is locally famous for its rickety boat ferry connecting the La Paz-side of Lake Titicaca with the Copacabana-side. The village is also where Pressly, my friend from the rabbit adventure in the Valley of the Moon, lived during the work week.

Pressly and I shared light work schedules which allowed us to take advantage of the lake and its surroundings. We hiked to remote shorelines and dove off rocks into the pristine yet icy-cold water. In the evening, we perched ourselves on rock outcrops and got lost in the most beautiful sunsets imaginable. Away from human touch, and blessed with expansive views, the purity of that place must have mimicked experiences enjoyed by humans from times past in settings around the world that are now familiar but have since become tarnished by progress.

Pressly lived on the second floor of a two-story structure. A man we dubbed "The Thinker," due to his quiet nature, lived beneath him. A trout fisherman by trade, this man tracked the stocked fish that had become a dominant species in the lake. He spent much of his time alone, weaving fishing nets.

Early one morning, ice formed on the edge of the lake. Expressing wonder at the sight, The Thinker asked me, "did this fall from the sky?" As the day was clear, and the rainy season several months away, it seemed he was unaware of the fundamental relationship between water and freezing temperatures. While perhaps a reflection of limited schooling, his curiosity was also genuine and enchanting. This ability to marvel at an ordinary yet still astonishing occurrence stands out as a favored memory from my Peace Corps experience.

LIFE IN BOLIVIA challenged me to attempt to contribute to people and societies that were seemingly in need. *Seemingly in need*—I emphasize this because my perspective was tainted by my values.

What I deemed to be abnormal or wrong most often was just different. While most Bolivians might have lived more simply than me, much of their condition was as they desired. Attempts to impose my or anyone else's standards on them failed.

Some of my fellow volunteers did succeed at bonding with and positively impacting their communities. Some went on to make lifelong connections with the people they worked with. Other volunteers, including me, may not have impacted Bolivia much, but the country undoubtedly influenced us.

CHAPTER 16
San Pedro

Families queuing to enter the San Pedro Prison, 2011

"The important thing was that we were alive."

—HENRI CHARRIÈRE, PAPILLON

S AN PEDRO, A gritty, middle-class neighborhood near downtown La Paz, is home to several landmarks including the Basílica de San Francisco. Constructed between 1743 and 1772 and adhering to a style architects describe as Andean Baroque, this monument is surpassed, in my view, only by Mt. Illimani as the city's most iconic symbol.

The colorful and extensive market outside of the basilica is another La Paz icon. It continues up the *calle* Sagarnaga, pivots vertically in the direction of El Alto, and then becomes the *Mercado de las Brujas*, or Witches' Market. This is the place to go for the sacrificial ingredients—llama fetuses, coca leaves, and other potions—used in a Bolivian *ch'alla* or offering to the Pachamama. The Witches' Market is also a good spot for photo enthusiasts.

ANOTHER EMBLEMATIC STRUCTURE is located a few blocks from the Basílica de San Francisco, even closer to downtown in the direction of the Sopocachi neighborhood where Ms. Silvya and her family

Llama fetuses for a ch'alla, *calle Sagarnaga, La Paz, 2011*

lived leading up to and during the Agrarian Revolution of 1952. The structure features an undistinguished exterior—an earth-toned wall which blends into the surrounding environment. Size, not detail, distinguishes it. Three stories tall, and said to be several meters thick, the wall envelops a full city block.

This is the perimeter surrounding *El Penal de San Pedro*, the country's largest prison. The entrance faces the Plaza de San Pedro, a destination for Paceños' weekend wanders and coffee sipping moments which they spend on park benches while watching their children play. Each day, a line of expectant visitors forms in front of the prison. The line typically extends along the distance of the front wall, and often around the corner. Some people are queuing to visit incarcerated loved ones. Others are there to sneak a peek at life inside.

Two tall metal gates secure the prison's entry. These lead to a small room where metal bars rise above a desk. Guards sit behind the desk to receive the public. After approaching, you are asked to state your business.

Just there for a glimpse? Then rush along.

A tourist with a little money to spare? Slow down. Don't be so obvious. Slip them a little cash, and you might be allowed in.

SAN PEDRO HAS been home to many of Bolivia's most notorious criminals, including Roberto Suárez Goméz, who as previously mentioned was portrayed as the Cochabamba-based drug lord in *Scarface*. Many other prisoners have played roles in the global War on Drugs, a crusade created by the US government but primarily fought in cities and rural areas throughout Central and South America.

Twenty-two years old and eager to experience things unknown to me, in September 1996, I set out to explore the San Pedro Prison soon after arriving in La Paz. As with the other visitors, I maneuvered the queue leading to the prison's front gate. After entering the waiting room—the space where the prison guards question visitors—I loitered toward the back of crowd to observe. The waiting room resembled a cage. Separated by windows lined with bars, packs of inmates congregated on the other side.

Noticing my awkwardness, one of the prisoners spotted an opportunity. "Speak English?" he whispered to me. "Meet English prisoner?"

Why not.

A few minutes later, a tall, black man appeared. As there were few people of African heritage living in Bolivia, this man's skin color made him stand out. His hard-to-place accent—British

English, perhaps with a touch of Caribbean—further distinguished him. He touched on the basics of his predicament. His name was Thomas McFadden. A failed attempt to smuggle cocaine out of the country had landed him in San Pedro. A Bolivian court had convicted him of this crime, but after several months, he was still awaiting sentencing.

A friend had recently gifted me the pair of sunglasses I was wearing that day. Supposedly, the glasses had traveled the world, exchanging hands from country to country. This seemed like a good opportunity to extend the regifting tradition. Delivering the glasses to Thomas inspired our short and memorable friendship.

My initial visit with him was brief. I never made it past the waiting room. Within two weeks, I returned with a new offering—a stack of reading materials including some aging *Newsweek* magazines that had been piling up in my apartment. (Peace Corps volunteers received a complimentary subscription to *Newsweek*. As I lived in Bolivia during the nascent moments of the Internet era, this was often my only consistent source of global news.) Thomas met me at the prison gates. He instructed me to hang tight and do my best to look relaxed. A few minutes later, he returned with a guard. After awkwardly slipping the guard a small monetary contribution, he allowed me inside.

My first steps past the entrance brought me into one of the prison's main plazas. Children played football. Men and women scrubbed their laundry. They hung their wet clothing, sheets, and blankets to dry on lines traversing the plaza, and over the edge of the balcony surrounding it. Coca Cola signs drew attention to storefronts where inmates hovered to conduct their daily grocery shopping. In another section of the plaza, a group of prisoners were busy building walls. These would become rooms for the next generation of residents.

Thomas McFadden, La Cancha, San Pedro Prison, 1996

I had read San Pedro described as a village within La Paz. I knew women and children were permitted to live inside due to regulations allowing families to stay together after a family member's incarceration. These people, their rules, and culture, constituted a unique society.

As extraordinary as the place was to me, much of what I witnessed mapped to my expectations. I found the feeling I experienced inside San Pedro to be the most unsettling part of my visits. A tone of despair hovered around the jail and seemed to infect all people inside. Escaping this feeling required freedom—the ability to depart at will—or the means to purchase an upgraded lifestyle while imprisoned.

Not all prisoners were treated equally on the inside. This seemed like an obvious conclusion. As in all locations around the world, San Pedro had its "haves" as well as its "have nots." Nevertheless, this circumstance provided an extreme example of income inequality. Poorer inmates received minimal rations, perhaps some bread and a bowl of soup each day. They slept on the floor of the prison's chapel, or in the alleys connecting the *comunidades*, or blocks, that comprised the jail. Wealthy inmates, including many of the drug smugglers, or *cocaleros*, had access to just about anything. Flaunting their *you-can't-touch-me* status, they erected satellite TV dishes on the rooftops of their apartment suites. Apparently, for a couple hundred dollars, they could even rent themselves a day outside of the prison.

Thomas took me on a tour. We visited the Los Pinos *comunidad*. Five bright stars painted on the wall at the entrance indicated this place provided some of prison's best accommodations. Children ran around freely while their parents sat at tables drinking tea and discussing current affairs. We went to La Cancha, one of the poorer *comunidades*. As its name implied, this was home to the prison's central football court. Again, kids played, but their laughter was stilted by inmates' shouts; their joy salted by the smell of urine.

After passing through a labyrinth of corridors, we made it to Los Alamos, the four-star *comunidad* Thomas called home. He invited me to his room which is where he shared his story.

THOMAS WAS BORN in Tanzania, but grew up in Liverpool, England. In 1995, he was caught in the El Alto International Airport attempting to smuggle five kilograms of cocaine to Europe. Despite encasing his packages in multiple layers of plastic, wrapping them in additional layers of spices and coffee, and placing all of this in a custom-made smuggler's suitcase—he was nabbed by a couple of drug-sniffing dogs.

He recalled, "After a few hours, guards transferred me from the airport to a narcotics office in La Paz. I spent two weeks there locked in a small, dark room sleeping on the floor without a mattress or blankets. I was cold, hungry, and thirsty."

Not yet able to speak Spanish, he banged on his cell door to get the guards' attention. In response, they used hand gestures to explain he needed to pay them to be fed. This was Thomas's introduction to the economics of the Bolivian penal system.

The next day, representatives from the British Embassy visited him. They provided him with some cash to cover his short-term needs. Two weeks later, they secured his transfer to San Pedro.

"Upon my arrival to San Pedro, I was taken to the prisoner registration office," Thomas said. "Guards immediately demanded a twenty-five Boliviano entrance fee. Because it was not my will to enter, I asked why I should pay. This only angered them. Not wanting to aggravate my situation, I promised to pay them the following day, after the embassy officers' visit."

"I asked about sleeping accommodations. The policemen quoted the prices of rooms in different prison sections. I found this hard to understand. Could I have heard them correctly? How could they expect prisoners to pay upwards of $400 for a place to sleep? I searched my pocket and found nothing. The police had confiscated all of my money."

Again, the British Embassy stepped in to assist. "They purchased blankets for me and provided me with additional money to rent a small room," Thomas said. "While the accommodations were simple, and filled with cockroaches, I recognized a significant improvement from the previous nights."

◆ ◆ ◆

DURING MY FIRST year in La Paz, I visited Thomas five or six times. When friends came to town, I brought them to the prison for a tour. A few of my experiences inside San Pedro stand out. Once, I snuck my camera inside. Advised to be especially discreet, I shot most of my photos from my hip. Few of these are noteworthy. I created a collection of shaky, over-exposed and poorly framed images serving as mementos of what would become an enduring memory.

During another visit, Thomas introduced me to a man he referred to as The Spaniard. Unsurprisingly, a drug offense had led him to San Pedro. I remember his rotten teeth and big smile, and that I liked him. He lived in an archetypal prison cell; a lone light bulb dangled from the ceiling. There wasn't a bed, or a desk, or any other furniture. Thomas later told me The Spaniard had sold all his possessions for drugs.

The walls of his cell were tinted a near-black orange; not colored with paint, but by age. Layered over these dark confines, The Spaniard had pasted clippings from magazines and newspapers. These images aggregated to create a purposeful montage. From one side of the room, a smiling model gazed to the other side where her glance intersected with the image of Goya's painting, *Saturn Devouring His Son*. It seemed the woman's look played a role in provoking the god's manic behavior.

The Spaniard showed me photos of his family. Classic dreams—a beautiful wife and two kids, a boy and a girl. In another photo, his daughter was riding a horse. Her long hair flowed in a warm Mediterranean breeze with the Spanish countryside expanding beyond. All of this gone, exchanged for chaos and fear; rotting teeth and an ever-present smile.

BY HIS OWN account, Thomas McFadden broke the law. He was tried and convicted. When I met him in 1996, more than a year after he had committed his crime, he was still awaiting sentencing. He was released from San Pedro in December 2000 after spending four and a half years inside. A few years later, he partnered with Rusty Young, an Australian who had also visited him in the prison, to publish *Marching Powder*, Thomas's account of life inside this most unusual place. Thomas now lives in Tanzania.

CHAPTER 17

From Goni to Evo

Political propaganda in the Altiplano, 2011

> *"I am not a liberator. Liberators do not exist.*
> *The people liberate themselves."*

—ERNESTO "CHE" GUEVARA

D URING MOST OF my time in Bolivia, Gonzalo Sánchez de Lozada, a member of the MNR party and a former Minister of Planning under Paz Estenssoro, served as the country's president. Well-distanced from the local political scene, I didn't pay much attention to his policies. The Bolivians I engaged with periodically accused me of sounding like "Goni," as they referred to their president. While born in La Paz in 1930, he attended boarding school in Iowa, and then the University of Chicago. His accent was more *gringo* than local, so my comparison to him was less than flattering.

Toward the end of my Peace Corps service, Bolivians elected Hugo Banzer Suárez to the presidency. Another relic of the revolutionary era, he had served as a junior officer under Silvya's father, General Humbertó Torres Ortíz, while he commanded the army's Fifth Division in Roboré. After his time with Humbertó in the jungle, Banzer's military career flourished. He received leadership training from the US military in Panama, followed by additional training at Ft. Hood in Texas. He served as Bolivia's minister of education, and later as military attaché to the United States. Adding to a familiar-sounding resumé, he returned from Washington D.C. to La Paz to serve as the commanding officer of the Bolivian military academy.

Committed to eradicating communist influence from Bolivia, and with some support from outsiders including Klaus Barbie, in 1971, Banzer led a coup d'état that toppled the elected president of Bolivia, Juan José Torres González. Four years later, while living in exile in Buenos Aires, Torres González was kidnapped and assassinated. His death is attributed to Operation Condor, the US-backed scheme intended to suppress left-leaning political groups across the Southern Cone. Banzer was implicated in this operation and in Torres González's murder, but never charged with a crime.

For the next seven years Banzer served as the self-imposed head of the Bolivian Republic. After receiving pressure from the United States—which itself had shifted from conservative to liberal leadership—he reopened Bolivia to democratic rule. In 1978, he attempted to manipulate the presidential election to his own benefit. A group of military leaders who had become frustrated with his leadership ousted him with a countercoup.

Out of office, Hugo Banzer formed a new right-wing political party, the Acción Democrática Nacionalista, or ADN. Under his leadership, the ADN remained visible but relegated to the opposition for the next eighteen years. In 1997, after much of the shade of his past had faded, Bolivians elected him to the presidency. An uneventful four years in office followed. The Bolivian economy struggled, and most of its citizens remained left out of any benefits from the country's natural resources wealth. His second term in office culminated with his diagnosis with lung cancer. In 2001, with one year remaining in his term, he handed the reins of government to his vice president, Jorge Quiroga. In 2002, Banzer died at age seventy-five in Santa Cruz.

Quiroga, another US-educated Bolivian leader, served for one year. In 2002, Bolivians elected Goni to a second term. Controversy marked his return to the presidency. Bypassing congressional oversight, he awarded lucrative gas contracts to foreign companies. The strategy of shipping gas out of Bolivia for processing removed the country from the most profitable portions of the petroleum supply chain. In 2003, citizen discontent peaked in an event known as the Bolivian Gas Conflict which resulted in the deaths of fifty people. This forced Goni out of office, and out of the country. For a stint, Bolivia's vice president, Carlos Mesa, stepped in to lead the nation.

Jorge Quiroga returned for the 2005 election, running against the socialist party candidate, Juan Evo Morales Ayma. Better known as Evo Morales—and like Madonna or Prince, commonly referred to with a single word, Evo—he was elected outright, earning most of the popular vote amid the country's highest-ever election turn out. In his success, Evo carried his people with him, becoming the country's first indigenous president. In his inaugural address, he proclaimed, "from five hundred years of resistance, we pass to another five hundred years of power."

A SON OF farmers, and himself a coca farmer and trade unionist, Evo rose to prominence as an antagonist of Bolivian neo-imperialism—the policies and people viewed as responsible for leaking control of the country's resources to foreign interests. Believing in the economic viability and cultural heritage of coca, he opposed US-backed efforts to eradicate its cultivation. Carrying forward the will of his MAS party—*Movimiento al Socialismo—Instrumento Político por la Soberania de los Pueblos,* or Movement for Socialism—Political

National flag of Bolivia (tri-color), adopted in 1851

Instrument for the Sovereignty of the Peoples as the party's long-form name—Evo initiated a wave of reforms reminiscent of the 1952 revolution. These included the ratification of a new constitution with a preamble stating:

> *In ancient times mountains arose, rivers moved, and lakes were formed. Our Amazonia, our swamps, our highlands, and our plains and valleys were covered with greenery and flowers. We populated this sacred Mother Earth with different faces, and since that time, we have understood the plurality that exists in all things and in our diversity as human beings and cultures. Thus, our peoples were formed, and we never knew racism until we were subjected to it during the terrible times of colonialism.*
>
> *We, the Bolivian people, of plural composition, from the depths of history, inspired by the struggles of the past, by the*

anti-colonial indigenous uprising, and in independence, by the popular struggles of liberation, by the indigenous, social and labor marches, by the water and October wars, by the struggles for land and territory construct a new State in memory of our martyrs.

—Translation by Max Planck Institute 2009

Among the constitution's principal components, the country was officially renamed The Plurinational State of Bolivia, reflecting the effort to enhance the status of its indigenous peoples. Bolivia adopted a second flag, the Wiphala. Its distinctive multicolored, woven pattern showcases the land of the Quechua and Aymara-speaking peoples of the greater Qulla Suya, a once unified territory extending across the southeastern Andes. It is an alternative and firm contrast to the traditional Bolivian tri-color banner which features a coat of arms guarded by a war-ready Andean condor.

Evo's government founded the new Bolivia on the principle of political, economic, and cultural pluralism. In addition to granting citizens the freedoms of religion and spirituality, the constitution

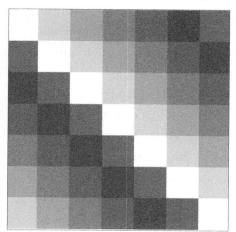

proclaimed all their languages the official languages of Bolivia. Spanish was joined by the languages of the rural native peoples, with thirty-six specific dialects mentioned in the constitution.

The country also adopted a selection of ethical principles. These included *ama qhilla*, *ama llulla*, and *ama suwa*—

Wiphala (Jhonnymollequispe, 2018)

declarations to not be lazy, not lie, and not steal. The concepts of *suma qamaña*, *ñandereko*, and *teko kavi*—personal commitments to live well, harmoniously, and full. Across all things, *qhapaj ñan*—direction or guidance to adhere to the noble path.

IN 2013, Evo surpassed Simón Bolívar, the first president of the Republic of Bolivia, as the country's longest serving head of state. Under Evo's leadership, the Bolivian economy performed well. According to the Center for Economic and Policy Research, real per capita GDP in Bolivia increased by 50 percent from 2005 to 2018, largely driven by global demand for natural resources, but also due to a prudent macroeconomic policy. (Andrés Arauz 2019, 1) Moreover, this growth placed Bolivia toward the top of the list of the fastest expanding economies in all the Americas. Some of the benefits of this expansion trickled down to the people. During the first decade of Evo's presidency, the incidence of poverty fell from 63 to 39 percent. During the same period, extreme poverty decreased from 39.5 percent to 17 percent. (Bolivia - Country Partnership Framework 2015) Evo's detractors pointed out, during his presidency, Bolivia remained the poorest country in South America.

Under Evo, the government also invested in grand public works projects. These included a cable car network that crisscrosses the La Paz skies. Named Mi Teleférico, this highest-in-the-world cable system extends from multiple points in La Paz, across the city, up to El Alto, and back again. The network cut commute times from an hour or more down to a predictable ten minutes. Everything delivered to the people for three Bolivianos, less than $.50, per ride.

While declaring itself a state committed to promoting the culture of peace, the right to peace, and to rejecting all wars of aggression, this new Bolivia has also continued to invest in its military. In 2016, Evo inaugurated the new "anti-imperialist" military academy in Santa Cruz. Officially named the Juan José Torres Anti-Imperialist Commando School, Evo dedicated this institution to the military general and former president who Hugo Banzer ousted from the country in 1971, and who became a victim of Operation Condor in 1976. (Juan José Torres was also the president responsible for expelling the Peace Corps from Bolivia in 1971.)

The new military academy preaches the unschooling of the nation from its colonial and capitalist heritage. During the academy's inauguration, Evo summed up this sentiment, "If the empire teaches domination of the world from its military schools, we will learn from this school to free ourselves from imperial oppression." (The Guardian 2016)

Evo's boldness appealed to some outsiders including the Cuban and Venezuelan governments. Expectedly, his policies also damaged Bolivia's relationship with the United States. In 2008, Bolivia ousted the US Ambassador, Philip Goldberg, accusing him of supporting rebellious groups in the country's lowlands. That same year, and for the second time since the program's inception in 1962, Bolivia asked the Peace Corps to leave. Emboldened and undeterred, Evo has proclaimed, "Latin America is no longer a Yankee colony." (teleSUR/MS 2017)

IN THE YEARS since I left Bolivia, massive demand for lithium, another of the country's abundant natural resources, has fueled anticipation for a new wave of expansion. A medical treatment for bipolar disorder, an ingredient for rocket fuel, and a base component of batteries in a wide variety of devices including smartphones and electric automobiles, this lightest-of-all-metals has expansive uses. The Salar de Uyuni holds one of the world's largest-known deposits.

Despite its potential, abundant Bolivian lithium has yet to deliver on the prospect of prosperity. Inefficient mining techniques, difficult to-reach mineral deposits, and fear by would-be purchasers to engage with a socialist economy conspire to discourage the interest of investors. Their attention remains largely focused on alternative lithium sources in Chile, Argentina, Australia, and elsewhere.

Land redistribution is another contentious topic. Before the 1952 revolution, property in Bolivia was unequally allocated, with the vast majority held by families of European descent who presided over large estates. In 1953, the MNR government under Paz Estenssoro established the Agrarian Reform Law, a program of expropriation and redistribution of rural land back to the indigenous people. Today, according to the National Agrarian Reform Institute (INRA), more than 50 percent of all surveyed and titled land in Bolivia is held by indigenous and peasant-led organizations, or by individuals or family farmers. Another 37 percent is titled to the Bolivian government, with much of this land set to be reallocated to the people. (Agraria n.d.)

Evo expressed desire to complete the project of land reform. Much of his attention focused on the Santa Cruz department and other low-lying territories, and the property held by powerful non-indigenous Bolivians. These groups asserted that their land— which in some cases had remained in a single family's possession for centuries—suddenly, and arbitrarily went up-for-grabs. Regulations permitted government bureaucrats to enter privately held property to conduct surveys, which could open the door to a reinterpretation of the land's ownership. In response, vigilant landowners sometimes took the protection of their property into their own hands, warding off the officials or indigenous squatters with guns and violence.

LONGEVITY BECAME CENTRAL to the debate surrounding Evo. Despite laws prohibiting presidents from serving more than two five-year terms, and from completing these terms consecutively, by taking advantage of loopholes, he completed three consecutive terms in office. This anomaly resulted from a 2016 referendum allowing presidents to serve a third term. While voters rejected the referendum, Bolivia's Plurinational Constitutional Court—the equivalent of the country's Supreme Court—stepped in to discard the results. In their judgment, the court cited the true will of the people, not the one these citizens expressed in their ballots. Evo, the clear beneficiary of this decision, ran for office again in October 2019.

Fueled by the dispute over Evo's political durability, the 2019 election was the most competitive in the country's recent history. Contenders included Jaime Paz Zamora, a former Bolivian president, Óscar Ortiz a standing senator from Santa Cruz, and Carlos Mesa, a historian and journalist who served as Bolivia's vice president under Goni, and then as president between 2003 and 2005. Leading up to the October 2019 vote, Carlos Mesa, emerged as Evo's most serious threat. After announcing his presidency, Mesa declared, "President (Evo) Morales is no longer part of the present, and much less the future. He is part of the past. He is the past." (Agence France Presse 2018)

To avoid a runoff election, Evo had to win at least 40 percent of the vote and beat his closest rival by at least ten points. Following the election, the initial vote count suggested he failed to achieve this threshold. Evo's 45 percent of the vote compared with Carlos Mesa's 38 percent. Bolivia's electoral tribunal continued their tally. Forty-eight hours after the election, and surprising many observers, the gap separating Evo from Mesa widened to the level required for Evo to avoid a runoff election. Stating, "the people again imposed their will," he abruptly declared outright victory. (Associated Press 2019)

Alleging a rigged vote, opposition supporters mobilized. They marched in the streets of La Paz, Sucre, and Santa Cruz. To suppress the unrest, police fired tear gas. Protestors responded with stones and Molotov cocktails. Several people died in the demonstrations.

One week after the election, Evo received an unsigned letter claiming to represent the views of 2,933 officers from the Army, Air Force, and Navy. The letter warned, "The armed forces of the state will never take up arms against the people. Our weapons will only be raised to defend our people, our constitution and our laws." (Mónica Machicao 2019) It's unclear if these officers were hedging their bets. They neither expressed support for Evo or the opposition.

Facing mounting pressure, and claiming he feared for his safety and the safety of his supporters, Evo resigned on November 10. He accepted an offer of asylum from the Mexican President Andrés Manuel López Obrador. From exile in Mexico City, Evo proclaimed, "While I have life, I'll stay in politics. The fight continues." (Lovett 2019)

The 2019 Bolivian presidential election resembled many previous elections, and the irregularity of Bolivian politics has remained a constant.

◆ ◆ ◆

IT IS LIKELY Evo's push for presidential endurance will damage his legacy. This may have also undermined democracy in Bolivia. Moving controversy aside, it is also fair to conclude, no other Bolivian politician since Simón Bolívar—not Humbertó Torres Ortíz nor Víctor Paz Estenssoro—did more to impact his country and his people than Evo. As the *Economist* magazine reported in January 2019, "Unlike other Latin American presidents with authoritarian leanings, Evo Morales has dominated his country less through coercion than through consent." (The Economist Group Limited 2019)

CHAPTER 18

Cordillera Real

View from my apartment in La Paz: Palacio Quemado in foreground,
middle-right, Mt. Illimani in background, 1998

"We all have our personal Andes."

—NANDO PARRADO, *MIRACLE IN THE ANDES*

B OLIVIA OFFERS AN almost complete spectrum of terrestrial climates. Arid, damp, Mediterranean, temperate, tropical, and tundra are all on display. During my time living in or visiting the country, I experienced many of these ecosystems. I witnessed explosive night skies from inside of ancient ruins on Isla del Sol. I trekked along pre-Incan roads down to the jungles of the Amazon basin. I experienced the San Pedro Prison from the inside. My two most memorable experiences in the country occurred during my last month living there. I selected these from a shortlist of my undiscovered adventures as a cap to my time in South America.

My life growing up around the mountains of New Mexico and southern Colorado provided context for the first of these experiences. As a child and young adult, I enjoyed exploring the Sandia-Manzano and Sangre de Cristo ranges that help define the southern tip of the Rocky Mountains. The prospect of experiencing peaks on a much grander scale played a significant role in guiding me to Bolivia.

The first time I landed in the La Paz-El Alto International Airport, almost immediately after clearing customs, I stepped outside to catch a glimpse of the neighboring mountains. My first find—the 19,974-foot tall Huayna Potosí. This Aymara name means "Thunderous Youth." According to local folklore, the mountain is the Lord of Rocks, as well as the first and most cherished son of the king and queen of mountains, Illimani and Illampu. Legend also claims Huayna Potosí guards the secrets of mankind in its core.

In awe of these mountains' sky-bending size and inspired by their legend, I moved to La Paz a few months after arriving in Bolivia. I was twenty-two years old. John Krakauer had recently published his *Into Thin Air* article in Outside Magazine. Perhaps the opposite of the intended reaction, his writing inspired my interest in mountain climbing. I was living in the right place; encircled by the beauty of the world's second longest mountain range. Healthy, energetic, and somewhat mountain-savvy, I felt prepared.

Of course, I was clueless. My eagerness characterized the outdoor inexperience Krakauer condemns in his story. But these were the Andes, not the Himalayas. Most Bolivian mountains required two to three days to summit, not weeks. Of all the big peaks in the Cordillera Real—those ascending above six thousand-meters— Huayna Potosí was known to offer the easiest path to the top.

Despite these breaks, I never made it to the summit. I attempted it once with two friends, Pressly, and Sarah. We rented crampons and ice axes in La Paz. Then we lugged our amateurishness and not-four-season gear to the base of the mountain. Bernardo, the husband of Peace Corps Bolivia's nurse, joined us as our guide. Apparently, he had climbed Huayna Potosí before, and he claimed to remember the route. No other member of our team had any ice climbing experience. From the moment we stepped out of the car at the bottom of the mountain, every step we took was the highest point we had ever climbed to.

After hiking through knee deep powder for a few hours, we arrived exhausted at an expansive and relatively flat glacial field in the shadow of the peak which loomed 1,500 feet or so above us. We claimed this as Campo Argentino, which is the high camp on Huayna Potosí. I don't know if the place we camped at was what we thought it was. As there were no other climbers close by and no markers on the mountain, we never verified the location. We had met up with a group of Spanish climbers a few hours before. They had pointed us in this direction.

The next day, Bernardo and I attempted to summit. Better informed by their experiences from our first day on the mountain, Pressly and Sarah held back. We left at 7AM, well-past the recommended departure time. Our route—selected from Bernardo's shaky memory—meandered up the face of an exposed fifty-degree pitch. Not quite a cliff, it was way too steep and slippery to hike up. We tried to tackle it with our ice axes, crampons, and obliviousness. That was my true initiation into the sport of mountaineering.

While the normal route up Huayna Potosí is supposed to be easy by alpine standards, some of the mountain's routes present first-rate challenges. The West Face features a three thousand-foot cliff. This forms a wall that shields the Altiplano from the humidity rising from the adjacent Yungas cloud forest.

Our route was far less extreme. Still, while tethered to Bernardo on that icy slope, I felt the humidity of the jungle. With my body pressed firmly to the mountain and my hands clutching axes, I shivered. I wasn't cold because I was surrounded by that warm cloud forest air. My trembles reflected the knowledge that if either of us slipped, or missed a hold, or smacked our axes into something unstable, we could easily fall. Our bodies would have fumbled down the cliff toward the origin of those misty clouds.

Less than one hundred yards from the summit, I pulled the plug on our attempt. Maybe we could have made it, but the risks outweighed the rewards.

FOR THE NEXT two years, I lived with this *defeat*. This isn't a great choice of words. I was never able to *win* anything. My goal was to experience the air and views from the top of an Andean giant. As I had not yet accomplished this, my time in Bolivia felt incomplete.

In May 1998, my last month living there, I gave mountaineering another try. This time, I focused on Mt. Illimani, the highest peak in the Cordillera Real, and the second tallest mountain in Bolivia after Mt. Sajama, the stratovolcano near the Chilean border. Illimani in the Aymara language means "Water Bearer." Folklore has established the mountain the king of the Cordillera Real, and the sentinel spirit watching over La Paz and the Altiplano.

Two of my friends joined this adventure. They included Mike, who a few months after the climb moved to New York to attend the Columbia Journalism School, and later worked for the Associated Press before becoming the director of communications for a major university. We were joined by Ken, a former Navy submariner who, a few months after climbing Illimani married a Bolivian woman. Eventually, they moved to Tennessee where Ken assumed management of his family's cattle farm.

Our adventure began with a drive from La Paz to the Zona Sur. We connected with a roadless path that maneuvered the same dry riverbeds, valleys, and canyons Humbertó had explored on horseback as a military academy cadet, eighty years before. After driving for a few hours, we arrived in Pinaya. At 12,000 feet above sea level, this tiny town marked the beginning of our climb. There wasn't much to it—just one road with a few kiosks selling sugary snacks to tourist climbers.

Passing quickly through Pinaya, we hiked on to the basecamp, called Puente Roto, which was in an alpine valley at 14,000 feet above sea level. We spent one night there. Removed from the city lights, we took in the Andean night sky with an array of stars best described as rare, or even sacred. The next morning, we continued our ascent. To preserve energy, we deployed a rhythmic hiking style with well-paced and purposeful steps. Ice, rock, and big skies surrounding us—we were trekking on the back of an ancient god.

The creator, Viracocha, designated Illimani the Lord of Water. The streams and waterfalls cascading down the mountain emanate from its glacier. Combined with ice melt from mountains across the Cordillera Real, this water is crucial for local agriculture. It is also the primary source of drinking water for the people of the Altiplano. We filled our bottles with it and treated it with iodine and sugar. Safe to drink, but unfiltered and retaining a brownish-yellow tone, this became our mountain tea.

On the second day of the climb, starting near Puente Roto, the route turned upward. We scaled a ridge of sedimentary rock. With each step, flakes of shale crumbled and then slid from beneath our feet. We arrived at the *Nido de Cóndores*, the Condor's Nest or high camp, in the early afternoon. At 18,000 feet above sea level and perched on a narrow geologic fold with the Illimani glacier on both sides, the camp provided space for around a dozen tents. We were joined by a handful of other climbers; teams from around the world who had traveled there to give semi-serious alpinism a shot.

By mountaineering standards, Illimani, as with Huayna Potosí, is not a difficult climb. Nevertheless, a collection of crosses lining the perimeter of the camp attested to its dangers. These crosses com-memorated people who attempted to scale the mountain but had never made it down alive.

From the Nido de Cóndores, the surrounding peaks of the Cordillera Real are clearly visible. They appear closer when witnessed from high altitudes. At night, the lights of La Paz glistened in the distance like the magma that once flowed from the mountain.

Deploying a basic knowledge of mountaineering gained from my botched attempt to summit Huayna Potosí, we awoke at 2 AM the following day. We collected our gear, strapped on our crampons, and headed out.

A narrow ridge of a hundred yards or so connects the high camp with a plateau. This presents some of Illimani's most technical climbing. Cliffs fall to either side of the ridge. We had headlamps to help guide us. Relying on 1990s technology that once seemed cutting edge, I failed to keep my batteries warm during the night. The below-freezing temperatures rendered the batteries and my lamp inoperable.

Light-less underneath the night sky, but tethered to my companions, I walked past many of the crosses I had seen the day before. Eventually, I stopped paying attention to the thoughts of what could happen if I stepped out-of-bounds. I could not see the danger, and so I became less aware of what I was supposed to be afraid of.

Memorials, Nido de Cóndores, 2011

Around 19,000 feet, Mike, one of my climbing partners, began to demonstrate odd behavior. He had once been a member of the varsity wrestling team at Cornell University, and he remained one of the strongest people I knew or have ever known. Despite his fitness, he appeared disoriented. Without warning and standing directly in front of me, he pulled down his pants, squatted and relieved himself.

Mike's bizarre behavior led us to suspect he suffered from cerebral edema. His climb was over. One of our two guides (we wisely hired professional guides for Illimani) connected a cord to Mike's waist, and short-roped him back to the relative safety of Nido de Cóndores. Within a few hours, he returned to normal.

Ken and I, along with our guide and one other climber continued. A few hours later, we witnessed the rising sun cast the long shadow of the great mountain across the Altiplano. Around noon, we summitted. The forever of Bolivian landscape—the entirety of the Altiplano all the way to Chile, and the Amazon basin deep into Peru—spread out before us. At 21,122 feet above sea level—that remains the highest point I have ever visited.

LIKE MOST PLACES on Earth, escalating climate change has taxed the Illimani glacier. Its eternal snows are disappearing. In 2017, a team of European researchers representing the Ice Memory Project led an expedition to the mountain. They collected ice samples for their physical database taken from some of the locations around the world that are most at risk from rising temperatures.

The scientists drilled into the glacier, more than one hundred yards down, to the bedrock surface that had remained covered and

From the summit of 21,122 foot Mt. Illimani; author first from left, 1998

frozen for more than 18,000 years. The ice samples they collected joined others in an ice library in Antarctica. This library represents windows into our planet's geologic history. While the knowledge of the library's existence provides some comfort, the tragedy is to know of the pending extinction of the real thing.

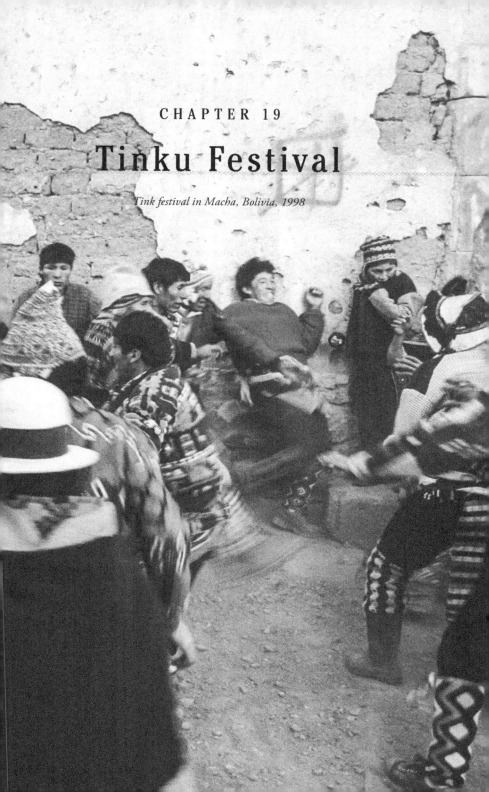

CHAPTER 19

Tinku Festival

Tink festival in Macha, Bolivia, 1998

"I saw neither sheep nor goats nor any other beast,
but I have been here but a short time, a half a day....
There were dogs that never barked....
All the trees were different from ours as day from night,
and so the fruits, the herbage, the rocks and all things."

—CHRISTOPHER COLUMBUS

FOLLOWING THE ILLIMANI climb, and with a few weeks remaining in Bolivia, I had time for one more adventure. I had heard stories of a fighting festival attracting congregations of *campesinos* to an obscure corner of the Altiplano where they would battle, sometimes to the death. Fueled by an inexplicable desire to watch other people injure each other, I joined a group of fellow Peace Corps volunteers and traveled to the town of Macha to investigate.

The Tinku festival originated in Potosí, but now takes place in towns across Bolivia. The word, Tinku, comes from the Aymara language, and suggests a meeting or an encounter. In practice, these "meetings" are ritualistic fights pitting men from rival villages against each other. Their "encounters" start with bold displays of color. Large groups of people from a village gather in a plaza. The men wear street clothes—blue jeans and button-down shirts. Their look is accented with brightly colored woven belts and gaiter-like ankle wraps. They also wear *chullo* hats, made from alpaca or llama wool, and featuring distinctive ear flaps accentuated with long tassels. Tied tightly around their chins or stuck in their mouths like a chomping bit, the tassels exist to ensure a snug fit. In place of a *chullo* or sometimes over one, fighting men may also wear a *montera*, which is a thick, leather-helmet-replica of something once worn by the Spanish as they conquered this part of their New World.

The women at Tinku are equally dressed to impress. Their brightly colored *pollera* skirts, vibrant shawls, and headdresses with long feathers ensure they are noticed. After all, attracting attention is a principal objective. The festival's pervasive dancing, singing, and fighting represent a form of theater, complete with romance and sacrifice—all orchestrated in honor of the Pachamama, the Mother Earth.

MY GROUP INCLUDED two of my roommates, Mike and Pressly. We met with others including Sally, who would go on to lead an architecture practice in Steamboat Springs, CO, and Bevin, the most jovial and boisterous member of our party, who would go on to become a college counselor in Portland, OR. During their Peace Corps service, Sally and Bevin were stationed in the Potosí department near Macha. They became our guides to the region.

In Sucre, we boarded an old school bus bound for Macha. The trip covered maybe 150 miles, yet it took ten bumpy hours to complete. Previous years' rainy seasons had damaged the roads. If these were in any town in the US, even if they were fire roads in the North American backcountry, local municipalities or forest services would have condemned them as impassible. For the Bolivian bus driver, maneuvering extremely variable terrain is a daily deed.

During the trip, passengers regularly had to disembark to allow the driver to tackle an obstacle. He was able to cross seemingly impossible chasms with the assistance of a few wooden boards, some boulders and a touch of luck. As with other drivers from across the country, ours could guide his bus to achieve levels of agility that anyone associated with its manufacturing at the Blue Bird bus plant in Fort Valley, Georgia would gasp with glee to observe.

The human intestinal tract is less forgiving. Several of my fellow travelers, the North Americans as well as the Bolivians, became ill. Proximity to the aroma of their vomit from the inside of a warm and dusty school bus became the catalyst for my discovery of oranges as an antidote to extreme car sickness. (Here's the trick—squirt the oil from a fresh orange rind directly into your nose.)

Slightly battered, we arrived in Macha in the early evening. Because most of us were under twenty-five and inexperienced with most things requiring planning, we had not secured, nor had we begun to investigate a place to stay. In our search for shelter, we began to discover the town. There wasn't much to see in Macha—a rectangular plaza with a clocktower at one end. Four streets branched off this main square at right angles. These continued for a few blocks, passing small quiet homes and storefronts, to the point where the town ended. It was just a dot in the middle of the Altiplano.

Someone from our group made a deal with a local school instructor. For a reasonable price, he agreed to rent us a classroom in the local schoolhouse. (The town had closed the school for the festival.) This large room featured access to a water well and a latrine. Over the next seventy-two hours, this would become our compound; an escape from the offbeat form of carnage that would soon commence on the nearby streets. Mostly, this find reflected young backpackers' ingenuity. With an extremely limited budget and the willingness to engage strangers without fearing rejection, we were able to find a safe place to sleep. This form of life-saving skill is easily forgotten as our lives progress, and our resources increase.

My memories of Tinku are assisted by photos. After paying a small fee—which likely was just a bribe to the local authorities—I received a "press credential." This purchase or bribe provided me with up-close access. Confidently or stupidly, I'd flash it to the local police and military officials—both groups were well-represented at Tinku—and then push my way to the front of the action. I captured all of this on film—the color, dirt, and blood that make this a tourist spectacle.

On the first day, joined by my friend Jay—perhaps the most multi-talented member of our group, he would later earn a PhD in linguistics, work for Microsoft, and then walk away from his tech job to become a high school Spanish-language and computer science teacher in Seattle—I climbed the bell tower in the plaza to watch the event commence. The festival began with a small group of people walking in a circle in the center of the plaza. Like a drain collecting substance after a rainstorm, more people were pulled in. The circle of humans swirled and grew to a flood. Then suddenly, the direction changed. As if the drain became uncapped, the marchers shot out in the direction of an adjacent street. They were out to pick a fight.

Jay and I climbed down the tower to follow the action. Like opposing forward lines on a battlefield, two bands from different villages met at a street corner. Then a pair of brave, or overly drunk, men stepped up to start the fight.

During the early hours of the festival, fighters adhered to rules. Their arms were expected to be locked and extended straight outward

People circling before a fight in Macha, 1998

past their shoulders. All punches were intended to be delivered from the side; dealt with an awkward swinging motion designed to limit impact. The police and military officials along with designated women from the village served as referees. Carrying whips made of rope, they struck anyone who veered outside of the fighting code.

Toward the end of the first day, these rules began to slacken. Village women appeared to hold tight to their roles as fight arbiters. They were there to ensure the Pachamama received her honors, and that the men from their villages walked away without too much damage.

On the other hand, the police seemed to relish in the spectacle. Like unhinged shepherds guiding their flock, they would strike at the crowds, pushing them in a desired direction. As dogs do when they are shown raw meat but not permitted to eat, they snapped at the fighters, stirring more violence which triggered more thrills.

By the second day, Tinku devolved into a drunken swamp. Walking in the streets, my friends and I were approached by villagers with requests for us to participate. These were uncomfortable confrontations from otherwise mild-mannered people who appeared to be attracted by the concept of adding a *gringo* to their combat resumes. We politely declined these offers. It's hard to say who would have won. Perhaps more than the participating *campesinos*, my group valued our teeth.

There are rules at Tinku, but as the festival progresses, these gradually disappear. Seeking the equivalent of brass knuckles, or a roll of quarters, fighting men began to pack their fists with rocks. When in need of more effective tools, some picked up boulders or bricks. When delivered to the side of an adversary's head, these objects caused pronounced damage.

People die at Tinku. I am not sure if this happened when we were there. We saw men splayed out on the streets, their blood draining into the cracks of the cobbled roads. Their injuries appeared to require critical attention, yet they were left there to sleep it off. There may have been a clinic in Macha. Maybe that's where the wounded fighters ended up. More likely, if they were to wake up, they would have received medicine in the form of another swig from a plastic bottle of pure alcohol.

Thrilling at first, the experience soured. Toward the end of our Tinku, we preferred to stay put in the schoolhouse. We went there to see something extraordinary. We wanted to cap our Peace Corps experience memorably. We did this but felt a bit less human for the effort.

◆ ◆ ◆

IN JUNE 2018, Bevin—one of the two women who had encouraged my group to go to Tinku—was diagnosed with a condition called Progressive Multifocal Leukoencephalopathy, or PML. Despite her vigor, and only three months after receiving her diagnosis, she died, leaving behind her husband and two young boys. Twenty-one-years after returning from Bolivia, Bevin was the first of my fellow Peace Corps volunteers to die. She epitomized youthful energy and abundant humor. While she was not a close friend of mine, her passing left a void for anyone who knew her.

Sally organized a memorial service for Bevin in November 2018. Twelve returned Peace Corps volunteers from Bolivia Group 14 met in Portland, Oregon. Most of us remain in contact with each other. Some of us are close, but group gatherings are rare. The two-decade-gap separating us from our lives in Bolivia has started to show. Wrinkles and circles have begun to appear around our eyes. Our bodies have grown rounder. Any short-lived experiences with malnutrition from our days in the Peace Corps training compound near Cochabamba have since been covered by our North American indulgences.

We remain an eclectic group of artists, architects, businesspeople, teachers, therapists, and non-conformists. Some of us are married, others are divorced or never found long-term partners. Some of us have children, others do not.

We seldom discuss politics. Perhaps this is because we have learned to question politicians' motives. A healthy sense of skepticism encourages us to doubt much of what we are taught to believe. While hard to pin down, this sense is a force that pulls us together. But it's more than this. A general curiosity to experience new things—the sentiment that led us to Bolivia—remains the thread that binds us.

The Saturday morning before Bevin's memorial service, we went for a walk in Portland's Kelly Point Park. On a small peninsula where the Willamette and Colombia Rivers meet, we gathered to share memories. Sally offered a prayer, which is a fitting tribute to Bevin, our group, and our common experience: "I am thankful for my family, who are my friends, and I am thankful for my friends, who are my family."

Of the handful of most impactful decisions I have ever made, choosing to move to Bolivia in 1996 resides at the top of the list of ones that have had the most impact on my life. By deciding to pursue the unconventional, and by relying on the flicker of confidence suggesting things would not only turn out well, but that life would be better because of the risk, I have led a fuller life.

I owe many of my most treasured friendships, including my relationship with my wife and our children, to that decision. As the years go by, the value of the experience matures. When I close my eyes, I can still feast on images, sounds and smells captured on icy Andean peaks, the streets of La Paz, and in the humidity-soaked Amazon jungle. My life is richer because of Bolivia.

Epilogue

Epilogue

NOW MOSTLY DISCONNECTED from her country's politics, Ms. Silvya returns to Bolivia regularly. Staying for as long as six months, she goes there to catch up with family and friends, for affordable medical treatments and checkups, or just to reconnect with the food, the mountains, and the air.

She and I connect frequently. Typically, I reach her by phone at her home in Fredericksburg. I imagine her sitting there, at her kitchen table, or in her living room surrounded by her art—the images and oddities she has collected from around the world. By touching, seeing or even smelling these items—including the Zanzibar chest of drawers she has hauled around for more than a half century—she is able to go back to the moment when the item first caught her attention. That is the perfect argument for investing in these types of mementos.

I recently asked her as I often do, "Why don't you come visit us next month?"

"Because I am busy," she responded.

I've heard this excuse many times before. She has things to do. "A lot of paperwork," she said. "There are bills to pay, and things that need to be organized."

This feels like a weak excuse. For all of us, there are things we are never too busy to take on. We'll drop what we're doing and quickly shift to these favored activities even if they result in significant cost. We do this because we love them. They are our pride.

Ms. Silvya is never too busy to return to Bolivia. The spirit of the place is too intoxicating.

MOST PEOPLE HAVE interesting stories to tell. Often, these are shrouded by everyday life. We coexist with our classmates, neighbors, and colleagues, or others who we pass by on the street each day as we head to work, or while we're standing in line at the grocery store. We take our mundane, everyday steps without pausing to begin to discover each other's uniqueness. After taking the chance to dig deeper, we can discover what we have in common is far more significant than what separates us.

This is the case with Silvya Gladys Angelica Torres Sanjinés. She was born in La Paz 1937, and for the past fifty years, she has spent most of her time in cookie-cutter neighborhoods in Northern Virginia. Her external appearance—everything from her conservative mannerisms to her home's orderly look—conceals a perfectly complex and fascinating life.

There is much to learn if we allow ourselves the space to discover.

Bibliography

Agence France Presse. 2018. "Ex-Bolivian president Mesa launches 2019 election bid." *Agence France Presse*, October 6. https://www.france24.com/en/20181006-ex-bolivian-president-mesa-launches-2019-election-bid.

Agraria, Instituto Nacional de Reforma. n.d. La Paz. http://www.inra.gob.bo/InraPb/paginaController?cmd=inicio.

Andrés Arauz, Mark Weisbrot, Andrew Bunker, Jake Johnston. 2019. *Bolivia's Economic Transformation: Macroeconomic Policies, Institutional Changes, and Results*. Washington, D.C.: Center for Economic and Policy Research. http://cepr.net/images/stories/reports/bolivia-macro-2019-10.pdf.

Associated Press. 2019. "Rioting erupts as Bolivia announces Evo Morales is near an outright win." *The Los Angeles Times*, October 21. https://www.latimes.com/world-nation/story/2019-10-21/bolivia-election-morales-opponents-riot.

Cervantes, Miguel de. 2016. *Don Quixote*. Translated by John Ormsby. Coterie Classics.

Coleman, Gerald J. 2015. *CIA World Factbook*. Washington, D.C.: Central Intelligence Agency. https://commons.wikimedia.org/wiki/File:Bolivia_Physiography.jpg.

Contreras, Manuel E. 1993. *The Bolivian Tin Mining Industry in the First Half of the 20th Century*. London: University of London, Institute of Latin American Studies.

2015. *International Development Association, International Bank for Reconstruction and Development, International Finance Corporation and Multilateral Investment Guarantee Agency Country Partnership Framework for The Plurinational State of Bolivia*. Progress Report on the Country Partnership, Washington, D.C.: The World Bank. http://documents.worldbank.org/curated/en/921771468186539912/pdf/100985-REVISED-OUO-9-R2015-0221.pdf.

Jhonnymollequispe. 2018. "Wiphala, Emblema de los Estados del Tawantinsuyu." *Wikimedia Commons.* https://commons.wikimedia.org/wiki/File:WIPHALA.png.

Laurence Blair, Dan Collyns. 2017. "Che Guevara's legacy still contentious 50 years after his death in Bolivia." *The Guardian,* October 5. https://www. theguardian.com/world/2017/oct/05/che-guevara-legacy-50-years-bolivia.

Lovett, Samuel. 2019. "UN warns Bolivia crisis could 'spin out of control' after nine killed in latest violence." *MSN.com,* November 17. https://www.msn.com/en-ca/news/world/un-warns-boliv-ia-crisis-could-spin-out-of-control-after-nine-killed-in-latest-violence/ ar-BBWTYMy.

Mahmod Ali Ayub, Hideo Hashimoto. 1985. *The Economics of Tin Mining in Bolivia.* Washington, D.C.: The World Bank. http://documents.worldbank. org/curated/en/312301468743379661/pdf/multi-page.pdf.

Marbilad-cwb. 2014. "Flag of Estado Plurinacional de Bolivia." *Wikimedia Commons.* https://commons.wikimedia.org/wiki/File:Bandera-de-bolivia.png.

Mónica Machicao, Ernesto Londoño. 2019. "Bolivia's Democracy Faces Pivotal Test as Unrest Spreads." *The New York Times,* October 31. https://www. nytimes.com/2019/10/31/world/americas/bolivia-election-protests.html.

Nag, Oishimaya Sen. 2017. *North Yungas Road - Bolivia's Most Treacherous Road.* WorldAtlas. https://www.worldatlas.com/articles/north-yungas-road-bolivia-s-treacherous-road-of-death.html.

Ortíz, Humberto Torres. 1937. *Campo Vía: Antecedentes y Consecuentes.* La Paz: Fenix - Illimani 66.

Read, Piers Paul. 2005. *Alive: The Story of the Andes Survivors.* New York: Harper Perennial Edition.

Sachs, Jeffrey D. 1989. *Developing Country Debt and the World Economy.* National Bureau of Economic Research Project Report, Chicago, IL: The University of Chicago Press, 57-80. https://www.nber.org/chapters/c7520.pdf.

teleSUR/MS. 2017. "Evo Morales: 'Latin America is No Longer a Yankee Colony'." *TeleSur,* December 24. https://www.telesurenglish.net/news/President-Evo-Mo-rales-Latin-America-Is-No-Longer-a-Yankee-Colony-20171224-0017.html.

The Economist Group Limited. 2019. "The movement to stop Bolivia's President Evo Morales". *The Economist,* January 18. https://www.economist.com/ the-americas/2019/01/19/the-movement-to-stop-bolivias-president-evo-morales.

The Guardian. 2016. "Bolivia opens 'anti-imperialist' military school to counter US foreign policies." *The Guardian*, August 17. https://www.theguardian.com/world/2016/aug/17/bolivia-anti-imperialist-military-school-evo-morales-us.

Translation by Max Planck Institute. 2009. *Bolivia (Plurinational State of)'s Constitution of 2009*. London: Oxford University Press, Inc., 6. https://www.constituteproject.org/constitution/Bolivia_2009.pdf.

Wikipedia. 2019. *Bolivia*. Wikimedia. https://en.wikipedia.org/wiki/Bolivia#Biodiversity.

Acknowledgments

THIS BOOK REFLECTS my personal experiences in Bolivia as well as conversations with a group of Bolivians who I am proud to call my family. These people provided first-hand accounts of the events featured in the story—from the common to the historically significant. I am particularly grateful for the many discussions I had with my mother-in-law, Silvya DeSousa. I am also grateful for the access she provided me to her father's written works. His book, *Campo Vía, Antecedentes y Consecuentes* and the manifesto he wrote from exile in Peru enabled me to remove the guesswork related to his perspective on some of the critical events in recent Bolivian history. I've endeavored to respect and honor Humbertó's legacy, and his family's heritage.

During a drive near the Santa Cruz mountains in California, Silvya's cousins Zonia Gonzalez and Miriam Braverman detailed the interior of their grandfather Crisologo's home in La Paz. Until that discussion, I only knew the house from its exterior. Zonia and another of Silvya's cousins, Gabriel Levy, also loaned me memories from their experiences as children living in La Paz during the 1952 revolution. Their perspectives added valuable details to my understanding of this event. Gabriel's anecdote of how his family saved the life of a cadet from the Bolivian Military Academy properly reflects the meaning in the famous passage from the Talmud, "... and whosoever preserves a single soul...to him as though he had preserved a complete world." My friend and Alice's cousin, Edward Lara, and Fernando Sanjinés, another of Silvya's cousins, helped fact-check some of the specifics related to the revolution. Fernando, who has also played a noteworthy role guiding contemporary Bolivian history, further encouraged me to recognize the complexity and multisided quality of war and politics.

I am also indebted to a handful of individuals who offered their time and skill to read and comment on earlier drafts of this book. Alice along with Jay Waltmunson, Noël Richeson, and Will Greene, thank you for your comfort with my many imperfections. Lynne Pearson, my copy editor, and Andy Ross, my developmental editor, thank you for your precision and constructively critical eyes. Domini Dragoone, my layout designer, thank you for thinking boldly.

I took most of the photos featured in the book between 1996 and 1998 when I lived in Bolivia as a Peace Corps volunteer, or in 2011 when I traveled there. Ms. Silvya and her cousin, Miriam, provided me with the others, a small treasure of photos featuring family members at various stages in their lives. In addition, I include epigraphs at the start of each chapter. Many of these passages come from books I read during the Peace Corps, or as an undergraduate student at Tulane University. Others come from writers, poets, and politicians who expressed sentiments that feel relevant to this story or the conclusions I am attempting to draw.

The nature of this book—which is intended to be an enjoyable, accurate and informative story more than a historical artifact—warranted a painting versus a photograph on the cover. Alice painted the image I selected. Her artwork depicts the Nevado Illimani, the sentinel spirit of La Paz, and I believe the quintessential symbol of Bolivia. Alice also painted the image of her grandparents, Humbertó and Alicia, and another image of her mother, Silvya.

These are featured with family photos toward the end of the book. As she did with my previous book, Sheila Edwards designed the front and back covers. Alice and Sheila, I am grateful for your creativity and support.

Finally, I am grateful to the Peace Corps and to the United States government for continuing to provide bipartisan support for this organization. At a stage in my life when my desire to better understand diverse cultures outweighed my professional experience, the organization gave me an opportunity to pursue a true adventure. The volunteer experience was what I made of it. Thank you, Peace Corps, for the chance.

About the Author

J EROME STEWART IS a writer, photographer, gardener, outdoor
sports devotee, and technology enthusiast. He lived overseas for
six years, including two as a United States Peace Corps volunteer
in Bolivia. He invokes these experiences, and his love of nature to
guide his writing and daily existence. He published his first book,
Standing on the Edge, Dealing with the Aftermath of Suicide, in 2015.
Raised in Albuquerque, New Mexico, Jerome now lives in Mill Valley, California with his wife, Alice, and their two children, Charlie
and Holland.

Dealing with the
Aftermath of Suicide

Jerome Stewart

ALSO BY JEROME STEWART

BLESSED WITH UNCOMMON wit and natural good looks, armed
with degrees from Brown and Duke, and engaged to a wealthy
investor, Maysie Campbell seemed to have everything going for her.
However, her outwardly faultless appearance and professional success masked deep inner turmoil. Her death by suicide in the summer
of 2013 shattered peoples' perceptions of her and initiated a process
of investigation and reflection by those who were close to her, including the author. *Standing on the Edge* is an account of Maysie's life—
how people perceived her, and how she viewed herself. This book
also traces the lives of three other people, all known to the author
by some degree, who likewise died by suicide. These four souls are
connected only through the similarity of their tragedies, yet their
families and friends are permanently connected through their grief.
The stories gathered here depict the evolution of healing—individual and non-linear processes that often carry unexpected outcomes
and insights. An interpretation of spirituality, fueled by natural
imagery—centered in Deer Isle, Maine, Orcas Island, Washington,
and Placitas, New Mexico—helps call forth an enhanced awareness
of the wealth encircling us all.

Made in the USA
Las Vegas, NV
01 October 2024